# *SPIRITUAL TRAVEL GUIDE*

By
Waldo J. Werning

Fairway Press, Lima Ohio

## DEDICATED TO

Pastor Art Beyer, Dan Grissom (Assistant to the Pastor for Small Group Ministries, who supplied creative and vital ideas for this book), and leaders of Trinity Lutheran Church, Lisle, Illinois, whose vision and action toward production of interactive Small Group Bible Studies made this "Spiritual Travel Guide" a reality. Their commitment to build believers through an Ephesians 4:12-16 and 2 Timothy 2:2 church model is the inspiration for the entire "Empowering and Mobilizing God's People" Discipling Series.

# TABLE OF CONTENTS

# FOREWORD

I believe that this book has been a long time in coming. I have believed and taught for many years the meaning and practical blessings of Ephesians 4:11-12, "It was he who gave some to be apostles, some to be prophets, some to be pastors and teachers, some to prepare God's people for works of service, so that the body of Christ may be built up." However, I lacked the instrument to implement this Word in the area of discipling disciples to disciple others. This book finally fulfills that vision and purpose for me.

I feel very privileged to have been part of the process that birthed this tool for the church. Watching Dr. Werning's passion for the equipping of God's people for spiritual service, together with the privilege of observing the excitement in members of Trinity, Lisle in using this material to bring the unchurched into the family of God and to train church members for that very task has been a once-in-a-ministry experience for me.

And more than ever I see the value of my ministry in equipping and training those whom God has placed under my spiritual care for small group and one-on-one discipling. More than ever I see this to be the model left for us in the New Testament. And more than ever before I am convinced that this multiplication of the ministry of the Word by the laity out in the community is desperately needed to fulfill the Great Commission today.

This Spiritual Traveler's Guide promises to help you faithfully do that. Use it with that goal in mind. And you will find that Dr. Werning has provided you with an invaluable tool for "making disciples."

Dr. Arthur H. Beyer

# Welcome!

Travel guides – how many times have we examined them to plan and anticipate a wonderful vacation? We may look forward to visits with relatives or friends, or have visions of snow-capped mountains, sun-drenched beaches, refreshing forests, bustling cities, rustic villages or a variety of experiences.

When you get where you are going, where will you be? Is that where you really want to be? Life is a journey of faith. How can you enjoy the journey of life as well as the final destination – heaven? This Bible study is about going the distance, reaching the goals and destinations which we set for our life, reaching all the way to New Life.

During the next 15 weeks, you will be seeking direction from God's Word to remap your own spiritual future as you travel down the road of life with Jesus at your side and the Holy Spirit guiding and strengthening you. This will not be a lonely trip, for you will be joined by a teacher/facilitator/leader in a group of fellow travelers (or some may be enjoying the journey one-on-one). You will discuss important aspects of your spiritual travel between two eternities, and you will look at the various signs you will see and events that may occur along the way.

During our personal study and sessions, we will spend special time to step into the presence of our Lord. It doesn't matter where we have been or what wrong ways we might have gone. We will hear a gracious and merciful God, who by His grace, invites us to walk and fellowship with Him. His abundant, steadfast love will be apparent every step of the way.

Because Jesus has taken the journey Himself, He reveals and shows the splendid destination He has prepared for us, and the abundant life He wants to give us here on earth until we join Him in heaven.

Good planning is essential for a successful trip. We must pick the best route to take, places to stay, and things to do along the way. Travel agents are there to help us. In a sense, the Holy Spirit is our Travel Agent, Who enlightens our minds and shows us the way to go. With the help of your teacher/facilitator/leader, consider the following suggestions for planning your journey which God has set out for you in order to make the next 15 weeks most profitable:

- Set aside a specific time and place to do your daily reading and study. Each week contains five days of study. Don't try to cram several days of reading into a single setting. This will frustrate and overwhelm you.

- Give yourself at least 15 or 20 minutes to complete each day's reading.

- Please write your answers to all the questions and assignments day by day. Be prepared to answer them in your weekly meeting with your leader/teacher. You may choose whether or not to share the more private and personal statements which you have written in your book.

- Begin and end in prayer. Only the Holy Spirit can direct and guide you in the learning process. Ask Him for help as you begin and thank Him as you end. Before you begin the study, please follow the suggestions for prayer below.

- Have your Bible available. You will be looking at many Scripture passages Reading them from the Bible will deepen your understanding.

Are you ready?  Shall we begin?

## Ask For God's Strength, Guidance and Encouragement

Before you begin your study, read the following Scripture passage and then pray for God to guide you.  A sample prayer is given.

> *"I will show you what he is like who comes to Me and hears My words and puts them into practice.  He is like a man building a house, who dug down deep and laid the foundation on rock.  When a flood came, the torrent struck that house but could not shake it, because it was well built. But the one who hears My words and does not put them into practice is like a man who built a house on the ground without a foundation.  The moment the torrent struck that house, it collapsed and its destruction was complete" (Luke 6:47-49).*

Father, I desire a firm foundation for my life.  I want to hear Your words and put them into practice.  I know how my own sin stops me and keeps me from Your plan for me.  Through your forgiveness of my sin by Jesus, empower me to begin this journey. Father, I ask You to strengthen me through the Holy Spirit.  Help me to be faithful in reading Your Word, to spend time regularly in prayer, to be conscientious in my preparations and to be open to Your voice as You call me to be Your child.  Protect me from the evil one, who would desire that I not take this journey.  Father, I ask these things in the name of Your Son, Jesus, my Lord and Savior.  Amen.

# WEEK ONE

# INVITING YOU ON A GREAT ADVENTURE!

Life is a great adventure -- at least it should be!  How would you describe your life so far?  Are you truly happy? Have you searched for answers in all the promises of the world?  Are you satisfied with the answers you have found?

Have you been successful in life or have you had serious problems? Maybe you would describe your life as average.  In any case, you are probably searching for a better way.  Something is still missing.  Perhaps you are tired of feeling empty. You hoped for more.

*Have you asked yourself, "Is this all there is?"*

## Day One – Traveling from Salvation to Purposeful Living

As a Christian, you have been given the priceless gift of eternal life in heaven with God.  He has claimed you as His child and adopted you into His family.  The gift of heaven is completely free.  We can do nothing to merit such love.  In response to this great gift of love, God desires that we honor Him with our lives. Too often we spend our lives trying to find meaning in things that please us but don't honor God.  Sadly, the results of such self-directed living rob us from the joy and fulfillment God desires for

12

us.  Many times we end up frustrated, wondering why things seem so "messed up."

As you respond in love to the priceless gift of eternal life, you will experience the true joy, peace and fulfillment that comes from discovering God's plan for your life.

On your journey of faith you will see change and growth in your life -- your beliefs, your values, your goals, and ultimately the direction of your life.  Your ideas regarding security, happiness and success will be challenged and shaped by God's Word. You will be strengthened by God's Word to overcome fear, anxiety, resentment, jealousy, boredom and irritation.  You will experience genuine contentment, trust and happiness in good and bad experiences.

Together with others, you will travel to new places of understanding, learning what directions to take, interpreting road conditions, and understanding God's timing for the trip. Throughout this experience you will examine and begin to live the truths that will help you to get the most out of your life's journey.

Your goal is to learn to see the spiritual reality of living as God's child.  Part of this reality is growing and maturing into the people God designed us to be.

In Hebrews 5:13-14 we see God's desire for us to grow up.  He wants us to understand His acceptance of us through His Son Jesus (our righteousness).  This gift from Him guides our lives on earth and assures us of eternity in heaven!  He says those not understanding of this gift are infants.  Mature Christians understand the gift and as a result train themselves in the spiritual realities of what God desires.

**How can you apply the truths of Heb. 5:13-14 to your life now?  How are you ready to grow up to maturity and a better understanding of God's plan for your life?**

Growing up to maturity requires that we learn to see that there is more to life than the physical, mental, material and geographical. These are vital in a limited measure for happiness in this world, but they are only part of what is real. Our deepest and lasting reality is found only in a relationship with the mighty and eternal God who created us through the birth process and recreated us through being spiritually reborn. The miracle of spiritual rebirth by the power of the Holy Spirit gives us faith and a relationship with God that grows and develops throughout our earthly life.

Our walk with God is a pilgrimage that will form the foundation for all of life's adventures. It is a reality of learning and knowing our true selves in our inner being with Christ living in us. It involves growing up to become who we really are in relation to the God of the Universe.

As you end your time of study today, go to God and ask Him for continued help to grow up to maturity so that you might be able to distinguish good from evil. After your time of prayer, spend a minute in silence. Record any thoughts you might have below.

## Day Two -- Going on the Road of Love

The path to understanding is the road of love that fulfills your purpose in life as designed by our heavenly Father. This love is not some single act of loving or even some series of acts. It is a dynamic condition which influences and directs all our thoughts, feelings and decisions. The source of this true love is God. Through His gift of love we are made new creations with our sins washed away. Through the Holy Spirit, God's love can now flood our lives. The human barriers that we erect to keep God away are shattered by forgiveness in Christ.

Do any of these barriers in your life keep you from experiencing God's love at this time?

- *A desire to control*
- *Poor relationship with parents*
- *Family problems*
- *Not forgiving yourself for things of the past*
- *Anger over past events*
- *Bad habits that control you*
- *Addictions or compulsions*
- *Sexual problems*
- *A drive for money and possessions*
- *Excessive anxiety*
- *Abnormal fears*
- *Past abuse that bothers you*
- *Disappointing experiences in other churches*
- *Life consumed by work, achievement and a desire for success.*

You may not be ready to discuss these issues yet. That's okay! Ask God daily to show you how to face your problems and grow strong as His child. God will work through issues as you are ready. Don't be afraid to let Him deal with matters that could separate you from Him. God cares about all areas of your life. His love for us can transform us by uncovering our sins and giving us the power through the Holy Spirit to overcome them.

Instead of being frustrated by patterns of sin, God wants us to rest in His love. Resting in God's love and sharing this love with our family and others is not something we achieve, but receive. As we receive His love we understand more of His plan and His expectations. As a result we look at everything with new

**WEEK ONE** 

eyes that have an eternal perspective instead of our limited world view. At this point barriers of sin come crashing down. We can enjoy God's love. We can forgive others and ourselves of past failures. God can work through us using this unconditional love to reach out to others. We can experience the greatest thrill on earth, being used by God for His purpose. Walking this path of love is the crowning point of our existence.

The direction and road on which God sends us on our faith journey is real, alive and lasts beyond our earthly existence and death. It gives us all the fullness God offers His creatures. Your experience for the next 15 weeks is power-food that fuels you for your life-long adventure with Christ living in you. Learn to organize your own personal itinerary for a life with God's purpose. The challenge for you is to plan for more than the ordinary journey and to travel the road of love instead.

Did God use your study today to show you things that might separate you from Him? Go to God in prayer and ask Him to encourage you with His forgiveness of all your sins so that you can grow closer to God. After your time of prayer, spend a minute in silence. Record any thoughts you might have below.

## Day Three -- Under God's Reign

*"But our citizenship is in heaven. And we eagerly await a Savior from there, the Lord Jesus Christ,"* (Phil. 3:20). Being a citizen of God's Kingdom, you will want to be strong and actively serve the Lord who rules heaven and earth. This will also require the difficult step of renouncing your citizenship in the "kingdoms of this world," which conflict with God's Kingdom.

As a believer in Christ, you will spend the rest of your life in God's Kingdom or Reign. As a result of your spiritual citizenship, keep thinking that you are a foreigner or stranger on earth and that heaven is your true and eternal Home. Now we are to grow in understanding our credentials, passport and visa to travel in this foreign country called Earth. We learn what we need for the journey and most importantly, what we can leave behind. We will learn much about the purpose for our earthly journey in the days to come. Our goal will be to discover God's power for living in His purpose.

In your physical birth, you were created with senses to function and interact with the world of people and things around you. God entrusted you with tasks that fit your skills and time. But your significance as a Christian is not based on your performance, but on your re-creation and being in God.

When you come to Jesus at the Cross, ownership of your life is transferred to God. As you grow in your relationship to God, you will want to go where God leads and do what He wants. You will still face difficult curves, treacherous ditches and dangerous obstacles on the roads you travel, but you will go with the brilliant light of God's Word and the strength of the Holy Spirit. Your "Travel Guide" will help you map your steps to move through the "ups and downs" of your daily walk in the Spirit. You will learn how much luggage you can carry, and to leave unnecessary things behind. You will refuse to be weighed

**WEEK ONE**                                                    17

down with things that distract you or hold you back from reaching your purpose and achieving your destination.

End your time of study by asking God to help you grow in your understanding of what it means for you to be a citizen in His Kingdom. Spend some time in silence after you have prayed. Write down any thoughts you might have during this time of silence.


## Day Four -- Building Relationships in the Body of Christ

The Christian faith is more than accepting doctrinal beliefs or church expectations. You seek to build a close relationship with the living God and Jesus Christ, Savior and Lord of your life. In addition to your relationship with Christ, you also need relationships with other Christians.

As you joined the family of human beings through birth, your Christian faith made you part of the family of God by a spiritual rebirth. You did not select the members of your physical family or your spiritual one. When you became related to God through faith, you became a spiritual relative of all Christian believers. This is more than an occasional family outing, picnic or party, but a life-long family journey or pilgrimage in the Church of our Lord and Savior, Jesus Christ.

The word "church" comes from a Greek word that means called-out people. The people in our congregation are called-out people of God. We can identify our church by the special relationship we have with God and with each other because we are all in God's family. While our building is important, it is not the church. Our church building is a place of corporate worship

**WEEK ONE**                                                        18

and teaching.  Our homes become the presence of the church in our neighborhoods.  We gather with other Christians in both places as we live out our faith and learn about God with members of His family, the church.

God has not only connected you with His Body - the church - but He has also given you a small group of other Christians who care deeply about your spiritual journey.  Life with your small group will provide many experiences of worship, community, learning, modeling, service and fellowship.  Participating in this group will greatly enhance your spiritual growth and development.  Enter into the experience with all your heart!  There will be people you can select as good models for your own life.  You will also be able to model for those who are younger than you in Christ.

Within God's church, there are many different levels of growth and maturity.  Our job is to provide a place where all people are challenged to continue growing.  Spiritual growth doesn't happen to everyone at the same rate.  As you participate in your small group, you will see people at many different levels.

*What are three levels of Christian growth identified in 1 John 2:13-14? What are characteristics of each level?*

1.


2.


3.

*In what areas do you need assistance from others to grow up into Christ?  (Check those that apply.)*

- *Examination of false teaching you may have received in the past*

- *Assurance of your salvation*

- *Ways to rid yourself of things that are slowing your growth*

- *Encouragement for struggling with problems*

- *The meaning of Baptism and the Lord's Supper*

- *Prayer for specific issues*

- *Other* _______________________________________

As you finish your reading today, ask God for help in developing a relationship with a person in your small group that has traveled ahead of you.  After your time of prayer, spend a minute in silence.  Record any thoughts you might have below.


## Day Five -- A Great Adventure

We want to be new and strong in Jesus.  Our goal for spiritual growth through study and discussion of God's Word includes gaining new *knowledge*, challenging our *attitudes* and changing our *behavior*.  Each week you will do one growth activity each day for five days.  It is very important to do the study each day.  Trying to cram several days into one sitting will frustrate and overwhelm you.  During your weekly meetings, you

**WEEK ONE**                                    20

can share how God has used your study this week to speak to you. They will be there to explore with you God's great plan for your life. Others will also offer encouragement, prayer and support.

Consider this "Travel Guide" to be a map for you to go on a Great Adventure for 15 weeks. Enjoy the support and fellowship of your small group as you seek a closer walk with God together. May the message and music of God's love explode within you to give you spiritual health and strength that impacts all those around you. May your presence encourage others to join you on the Great Adventure!

## My Expectations and Commitment

Spend a moment to complete the questions below. Remember you are making a commitment. Enter into this commitment with anticipation of what God will do in your life. Ask God to give you the strength to keep the commitments you are about to make.

1.      What do you hope to gain by taking this spiritual journey?


2.      Please make a Promise/Covenant with God and those with whom you are studying these truths about God:


My Promise:
- I will pray to God at all times asking Him to be my Teacher and Guide for this journey.

- I will complete my work of reading the daily and weekly pages, and answer the questions.
- I will attend Worship Services weekly.
- I will attend my small group meeting weekly.
- If I have any special questions or needs, I will contact my facilitator/leader.

______________________________________

My signature

Go to God in prayer and ask Him for the strength to complete this journey. After your time of prayer, spend a minute in silence. Record any thoughts you might have below.

## Major Points for Review

1. God has given a priceless gift of forgiveness and eternal life through Jesus Christ. Can you describe what this gift means to you?

2. God wants you to grow up and mature as a Christian. There are barriers in Christian growth that must be challenged and overcome through God's power. How do you need help for overcoming any barriers today?

**WEEK ONE**

3.  To grow up in Christ means that we are ready to live under His reign.  We recognize that we are traveling through a foreign country while on this earth and our real home is heaven.  What are your hesitations in leaving the kingdoms of the world?

4.  You will need the help of other Christians on your journey. What will be the most difficult part of your participation in a small group?

## OBSERVATIONS/REFLECTIONS ON WHAT YOU STUDIED THIS WEEK:

**1.  What matters or issues would you like to know more about?  What, if anything, troubled you about what you studied?**

**2.  What new knowledge or insights have you learned?**

**3.  How has your faith grown or been modified?**

**4.  How will this affect your life?**

# WEEK TWO

# HOW DO I GET FROM HERE TO THERE?

Your Great Adventure starts by recognizing where you are right now. Through the Word, God will tell you how to walk and live with Him. He is the One who gives you all things, including your happiness and security. Knowing you're "here"(present spiritual location) and going "there" (your earthly and eternal destination) gives you the proper perspective on life's travel and the one who will guide you, God.

## Day 1 -- Where Are You?

"Where are you?" The God of the Scriptures asked this searching question of Adam and Eve (first two human beings in history) in the Garden of Eden. Genesis 3:9-22 tells the tragic account of God's creatures living in a beautiful place created for them, then disobeying their Creator by eating of the one tree forbidden to them. This act was against God's will. Their sinful act was followed by their hiding from God. When God came to them, they hid because they were naked, having lost their innocence. Shifting blame, Adam faulted Eve, who accused the serpent. This is the "blame game," which we all have inherited.

Genesis 1:14-19 records the curse that all the human race experienced because our original father and mother sinned by disobeying God. Adam and Eve thought they knew what was best for them. They ignored God's specific instructions.

Sin can be defined as either by failing to do what God requires or doing what He forbids. Sin can be a thought (1 John 3:15), word (Matthew 5:22), or deed (Romans 1:32).

*Read Genesis 3:9-22, and tell what they did wrong.*




*How do people choose to ignore God's instructions today? What are the consequences?*




From Adam and Eve's time, people have known good and evil. Since then, the Devil (who is the author of evil/rebellion/disobedience) has fought against God, who is holy, just, and perfect. The Great Liar/Tempter is also our worst enemy. He constantly lures us to be where we should not be and to do what is wrong.

*The question today is still the same, "Where are you?" Are you hiding from God?* Are you where God wants you to be, doing what God wants you to do? Are you with those who will help, not hinder you from reaching the earthly and eternal destination that is good for you? Do you know the places God wants you to reach?

Are you taking time for your spiritual mapping and travel plans so that you move along with God, no matter what your situation may be? Are you prepared to go the distance to reach and pass over and through the mountains, valleys, plains and seashores to which God is calling you? Or maybe you have been

**WEEK TWO**                                                    **25**

following your own plan for your life without regard to God's plan.

*How have you experienced the consequences of your own sin?*

God's call to us is to desire Him and obey His will. When we recognize the glory of being a child and heir of God's kingdom, we will find joy in embracing Him and doing His will. Christ said, "...I seek not to please Myself, but Him who sent Me" (John 5:30). Like Jesus, our purpose on earth is also to do what our Heavenly Father desires.

We have several options, for God does not force His will upon us. We can run away; we can do nothing, going the way of self-will; or we can do it God's way, which keeps us living in His love. This may alienate us from people who reject Christ and/or our Christian values.

The fantastic thing is that wherever God leads us to go, His grace and love will help and strengthen us to go and do what will bring us good and joy. It is important that you understand the term grace. It is used extensively in this book, but most importantly, it is the foundation of your life as a Christian. Grace is favor or kindness shown without regard to the worth or merit of the one who receives it and in spite of what that same person deserves. The only way of salvation for any person is "through the grace of the Lord Jesus Christ" (Acts 15:11). Grace is also God's power given us to do good and to serve Him.

As God asks, "Where are you?," remember that this is a question of a loving Father. He wants you to walk the way that brings you true happiness, security and success, and then eternal companionship with Him. God's grace allows us this access to Him through His Son, Jesus.

**WEEK TWO**

We do have a choice about where we should be and where we need to go. We can follow our father Adam and mother Eve, who were chased out of the Garden of Eden, and then stumbled and wandered through unknown terrain and relationships. We are the heirs of their stumbling. On the other hand, our Father God invites to us to follow Him on a pilgrimage that gives us a life that transforms our living now and also leads to the eternal garden called Heaven.

*What does it mean to follow our Father God? Why should we wish to follow Him? What are the consequences?*

As you finish today's study, spend a minute in prayer, asking God for wisdom to make choices in all areas of your life that will honor Him. After your time of prayer, spend a minute in silence. Record any thoughts you might have below.

## Day 2 -- Change To Another Direction

We go where our minds and hearts tell us to go. Our beliefs direct our ways. This is true of our spiritual lives as well as physical. This means that our religious beliefs, attitudes and values determine the direction and speed we will travel. Our mental map makes the big difference in how successfully we travel and whether we end at the right destination. What's inside us will determine what we experience outside.

*How would you characterize the direction of your life to this point? Why?*

- *Right on target*

- *All over the map*

- *Lost in the woods*

- *Ready for mid-course corrections*

Many people think they will be happier if they can change their landscape and external environment. However, how you are on the inside directly affects the way you will answer the questions, "How are you? What direction are you going?" What happens in your inner spirit, mind and heart generally determines more than anything else how you are and where you will choose to go.

The list below contains many different directions people choose. In following these "directions" many people think they receive ultimate happiness. Have you tried finding your happiness in any of these as your priority in life?

- Money/Stocks
- Fame
- Promotions
- Fitness
- Losing or gaining weight
- New house
- Good retirement
- Comfortable life
- Owning your own business

People may have lots of things and many relationships -- wealth, health, leisure, a good job, good friends, etc., and yet be very miserable. A sense of worthlessness, failure, guilt, and fear result from bad beliefs, attitudes and behaviors.

Renewal of our mind and heart by the Spirit of God through forgiveness by Jesus' blood creates deep changes in the innermost recesses of our person. The Holy Spirit recreates our

**WEEK TWO**  28

inner environment so that we may travel successfully in outside landscapes, whether easy or difficult.

The rich fool who tore down barns to build bigger for selfish physical and material satisfaction forgot the needs of his soul, as he elevated the earthly and diminished the eternal (Luke 12:16-21). Often people like him see reality through things they can touch and possess. Values that are restricted to the physical and material will greatly limit our possibilities for true happiness and security.

Many wrongly see the Christian faith and discipleship to be a behavior pattern instead of an inner regeneration that flows from the inside to the outside. This can be seen as we look at this graph representing our world view or reality:

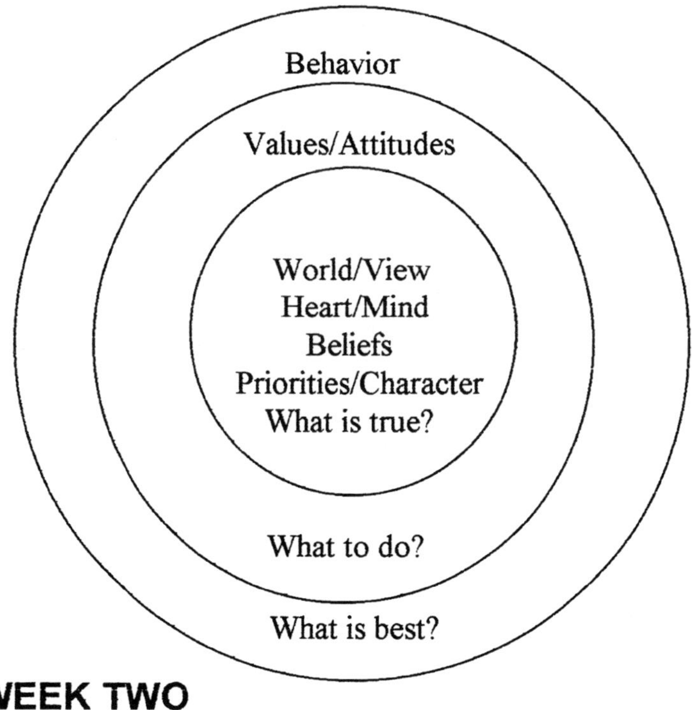

Whatever is in our inner being -- beliefs, values and attitudes -- becomes our mental map or world view, the way we look at things, and how we plan our spiritual voyage. WE CHANGE FROM THE INSIDE OUT, NOT THE OUTSIDE IN. Our behavior is a reflection of our beliefs and values. Jesus spoke this truth clearly in Mark 7:20-23.

*What is the main point of Jesus' words?*

*What does it mean to be changed "inside/out"?*

*Why is it important to know that we change from inside out rather than outside in?*

Our attitudes can only be changed by a change of our minds and hearts, and beliefs. Our old nature hates change. It causes us to fight against looking inside honestly because it is too threatening and frustrating to face the necessity of deep internal change. We want to accept only what we can manage and control rather than penetrate into our deeper recesses and make fundamental changes. We are tempted to live with the delusion of doing the right thing by correcting our ways just a little bit to ease our consciences.

*Do you think your spiritual life requires fundamental change?*
*Why or why not?*

      It is much easier to dust off the surface of our lives than to endure the inner cleaning process of spiritual change and repentance.  Repentance calls us to say we are sorry, then to turn away from offensive behavior.  This cleaning process of forgiveness takes out the poisons that are destroying us.  We would rather say 100 times that we are sorry, or "The devil made me do it", than sincerely repent and  change.  If we truly repent of a sinful act, we gain inward renewal by the blood of Jesus.

      Since our behavior comes from what is inside, we should examine what is there now and how it got there.  What beliefs and values have you accepted to be true? Have you ever considered the source of your current values?  Where did they come from? Chances are that you have been collecting them from people and experiences since birth. You collected most of them without realizing that you were doing so!

*Where did you get the following belief/attitude/value?*

| Belief/Attitude/Value | Source or Origin |
| --- | --- |
| Honest work | |
| Angry or peaceful? (Circle one) | |
| Holding grudges or easily forgiving (Circle one) | |
| Mature love | |

| Self-control or lack of it? (Circle one) | |
| --- | --- |
| Praying to God in Jesus' name | |
| Caring for others | |

*Generally, does your daily behavior come more from being a son/daughter of Adam (human being) or more of being a son/daughter of God?*

Wrong beliefs and values result in improper expectations for our lives. Do you let your happiness depend upon people and events? The outside world of events brings joy and peace only for fleeting moments. We must let God work in our hearts to show us His values for our lives. As we grow in this understanding, our whole definition of our lives, our purpose and the basis for our happiness will change.

As you finish your reading for today ask God to show you the source of your values. Ask Him to identify those values that are in conflict with His plan for your life. After your time of prayer, spend a minute in silence. Record any thoughts you might have below.

## Day 3 -- Growing In Belief In The True God

You were created to function in this world by the use of your mind.

*The big question is: What beliefs fill your mind and give emotion to your heart and thus cause you to do what you do and go where you go?*

God has made you a person responsible to make choices. You are entrusted with skills and abilities to do tasks for God and others. You are a unique person. Your significance is not based on your performance. This is Satan's delusion. God's Word shows you that your significance comes from being a child of the heavenly Father by faith in Jesus Christ. That Christian belief should direct your life.

*Which of the statements below best characterize how you see God?*
- *Policeman*
- *Kind old man*
- *Loving, caring father*
- *Forgiving*
- *Judge*
- *Other*

_________________

Believing/belief is the explosive factor or dynamic in your life, which changes bad attitudes/actions to good. First, true belief gives us salvation: "Believe on the Lord Jesus Christ, and you will be saved..." (Acts 16:31). Salvation does not come from anything that we do, but comes from what God has done in our mind and heart: "It is with your heart that you believe and are justified. It is with your mouth that you confess and are saved" (Romans 10:10). It's what comes out of your mind and heart that makes the difference.

**WEEK TWO**                                    **33**

*What connection is there between your beliefs and your attitudes/values and behavior?*

Satan will try to deceive us with false beliefs, so that we accept lies about God rather than the truth. Satan wants us to have a lack of understanding of who God is so he can control us. Instead, through Jesus' love, "from the beginning God chose you to be saved through the sanctifying work of the Spirit and through belief in the truth"(2 Thes. 2:13). Our Christ-focused beliefs keep us obedient to God on our way through life: "His divine power has given us everything we need for life and godliness through our knowledge of Him who called us by His own glory and goodness. Through these He has given us His very great and precious promises, so that through them you may participate in the divine nature and escape the corruption of the world caused by evil desires" (2 Peter 1:3-4).

Remember, change of behavior and of relationships always begins with a change of knowledge, understanding and attitudes -- which constitute our beliefs. Renewal of our thinking is basic to obeying God: "Do not conform any longer to the pattern of this world, but be transformed by the renewing of your mind. Then you will be able to test and approve what God's will is -- His good, pleasing and perfect will" (Romans 12:2). Our deceitful desires and sinful habits will be changed only "by the renewing of our minds" (Eph. 4:23). Our minds are renewed through intake of the Word, prayer, worship and fellowship.

**WEEK TWO** 34

*How is the mind "renewed"?  Why is "renewal of our mind" regularly a necessary spiritual exercise?*


*What beliefs do you need to evaluate and reconsider during these weeks of your spiritual travel?  Which of your beliefs need more investigation or reinforcement?*


Go to God now in prayer and ask Him to guide you as consider the things you hold as truth.  Ask Him to lead you to His truth and away from the false beliefs the world holds up as truth.  After your time of prayer, spend a minute in silence.  Record any thoughts you might have below.


## Day 4 -- Gaining Better Attitudes/Values

Christianity is not only about beliefs and salvation, but also about living the Christian life.  We go from saving faith to a life that expresses our faith.  Because of the great promises of God, you are urged to:  *". . . make every effort to add to your faith goodness; and to goodness, knowledge; and to knowledge, self-control; and to self-control, perseverance; and to perseverance, godliness; and to godliness, brotherly kindness; and to brotherly kindness, love.  For if you possess these qualities in increasing measure, they will keep you from being ineffective and unproductive in your knowledge of our Lord Jesus Christ" (2 Peter 1:5-8).*

These qualities are part of our character and attitude/values that impact our lives. They guide us in our daily excursions into our personal world.

In addition to these types of qualities, our belief in God will also shape our values. Prominent characteristics of Christian values/ethics are:

1) wanting to do the will of God;
2) having godliness by seeking the character of God as the pattern for our character;
3) loving without expectation of return, for God's love is unconditional;
4) living in covenant with God, who set specific obligations in faith for His people;
5) being involved in the Christian community, not isolating ourselves.

***Which of the qualities above do you lack or find are weak in your life?***

Possibly, after reading about character qualities and values you feel you could never live up to such expectations. You are right! By yourself, you won't be able to overcome the sinful tendencies in your life. God has a plan by which the Holy Spirit desires to change your beliefs and ultimately your values and behavior. As God works to shape your beliefs, your life will change. As a result, you will begin to measure all aspects of your life with a new standard that comes from God.

Throughout this process of being changed by God, we must remember these important points:

1.  *God's favor is not dependent on our goodness.* Jesus' death has given us our relationship with God, and it is not based on our ability to please God with our behavior. We have been adopted as God's children.

2.  *Our motivation to follow God's plan comes from our understanding of His unconditional acceptance of us.* We are responding to the gift of eternal life freely given us. Any other motive will not honor God.

3.  *God by His grace changes us into new people and gives us strength to live by the Spirit to follow His requirements for our lives.* We ask God to change us from the inside out.

As we come to a fuller realization of these points, we can increasingly base our self-image on who God says we are and not on our ability to perform. In that way God gives us rest and peace from trying to prove ourselves to Him and to others.

The way we view and value ourselves will determine the direction of our lives. A wrong standard of values will drive us in the wrong direction. The Christian heart pursues and pays attention to what it cherishes and provides, and protects what it values.

Devaluation of life is an expression of sin, for sin distorts value as it changes the price tags. Devaluation of people can always be traced to a reduction of God. After refusing to glorify God, some people "...exchanged the truth of God for a lie, and worshipped and served created things rather than the Creator..."(Romans 1:25).

Love needs an anchor, and the only stable foundation is Christ. Christian values differ radically from all others because God is seen as the ultimate source of truth and authority, and Jesus Christ as Lord of all areas of life. God's standards are our blueprint for living. Someone has said, "Sow a thought, reap an act; sow an act, reap a habit; sow a habit, reap a character; sow a character, reap a destiny." Love is our destiny.

Even if we keep our distance from God so that He does not penetrate too deeply, He does not kept His distance from us. He is ready to open our eyes to whatever is true, however unsettling it may be. He will replace our pretended satisfaction and false certainty with real Christian faith, hope, and love.

Your Father in Heaven desires that your values and attitudes reflect His love. The beginning point for these changes in your life is growing in your understanding of God's love for you. Go to God in prayer and ask Him to show you clearly how much He cares for you. Tell Him you would like to reflect His values and attitudes with your life. After your time of prayer, spend a minute in silence. Record any thoughts you might have below.

## Day 5 -- Right Beliefs and Attitudes Produce Right Behavior

Jesus is never satisfied with mere religious "talk." He desires fruit on the tree -- properly motivated actions that prove the sincerity of what we say and the reality of our belief. *"Therefore show these men the proof of your love and the reason for our pride in you, so that the churches can see it"* *(2 Cor. 8:24).*

Paul asserts that active service and giving is a "proof of our love." Christian faith is to be expressed in good works. Jesus wants fruit, not excuses for failure to produce a crop of good works.

God's attitude toward a Christian life without action is shown by His curse of the fruitless fig tree (Luke 13:6-7).  The fig tree, planted in the orchard to bear fruit, failed totally in the purpose for which it existed.  It is a great tragedy when Christian lives are empty of the produce of their Christian faith.  Jesus showed this clearly when He asked in Luke 6:46, "Why do you call me, 'Lord, Lord,' and do not do what I say?"

Once again we are presented with a call to carry out God's plan.  We are following God's plan for us because we are saved.  God desires us to do what He asks, for the right reasons.

*What is your motivation for acting on God's desires for your life?*


An old truth repeated often affirms, "The longest distance in the world is the space between the mind and the heart." This emphasizes the importance of transferring what we believe and think into a willingness to act.  Someone said, "To know and not to do is yet not to know." Failure to act upon what we know to be right is a denial of the truth we hold.  Jesus said it in a positive way, "Now that you know these things, you will be blessed if you do them" (John 13:17).

Jesus also said, "Blessed rather are those who hear the Word of God and obey it" (Luke 11:28).  He emphasized this in much stronger terms when He stated that those who obey Him in their spiritual lives are closer to Him than His physical mother and brothers, "My mother and brothers are those who hear God's Word and put it into practice" (John 8:21).

*Are there other barriers that might prevent you from going full speed in your study/travel during the remaining 13 weeks?*

**WEEK TWO**                                   **39**

*What special efforts will be required for you to overcome all learning disabilities in embracing God's teachings?*

You can readily recognize that a study of God's Word together with others in this "Spiritual Travel Guide" is not just for informing you about the way of salvation. Your study is also about transforming your attitude, character and actions to walk faithfully on the spiritual road which God wants you to walk. Filling your head with divine facts is just the first step to gaining the fullness of life in Jesus. To have Jesus as Lord of your life means first a knowledge of God and a belief in Jesus Christ for salvation, and then an attitude of response, wanting Christ fully formed in you and living for Him faithfully. This means properly motivated behavior that is an expression of your faith in Christ.

Our deeds do not earn salvation, but they are done by us as Christians by the power of the Holy Spirit to share God's love. So James says, *"...Faith by itself, if it is not accompanied by action, is dead" (2:17). "Do not merely listen to the word, and so deceive yourselves. Do what it says" (James 1:22).*

Christian faith without doing good works by the power of the Holy Spirit is a dead faith, worth nothing. God's Word and discussions during these weeks are both for informing you and transforming you.

Jesus said, "If anyone loves Me, he will obey My teaching" (John 14:23). This obedience is not to make us more certain of our salvation or to make us more saved. It is an obedience of faith. That's what this day's lesson is all about. We are assured of a loving and intimate relationship with our heavenly Father through His Son, Jesus Christ, our Savior and

Lord now and forever. Because of this wonderful gift, we respond in action.

It is one thing to know something and a totally different thing to take action on what you know. God desires action on your part. Pray now and ask God to give you the strength to act on what you know. After your time of prayer, spend a minute in silence. Record any thoughts you might have below.

## Major Points for Review

1. What is the relation between faith and action?

2. Our sin has separated us from God. As a result we suffer the consequences of sin in our lives. What is the ultimate consequence of sin?

3. In order to move towards God's plan for our lives, we must let God shape and mold our inner most beliefs and values. How are you ready to explore God's plan for your life?

4. Our behavior is shaped by our innermost beliefs and values. Which of your inner beliefs and values are you most afraid to let God change in accordance to His plan?

5. The motivation to undertake this change is God's unconditional acceptance of us. How has this truth affected your journey of faith?

6. What are some changes in behavior that you will consider and about which you will talk to God?

## OBSERVATIONS/REFLECTIONS ON WHAT YOU STUDIED THIS WEEK:

1. What matters or issues would you like to know more about? What, if anything, troubled you about what you studied?

2. What new knowledge or insights have you learned?

3. How has your faith grown or been modified?

4. How will this affect your life?

# WEEK THREE
# WHO IS GOD AND WHAT IS HE LIKE?

We earthbound creatures get so busy and glued to our daily work, activities and those around us that it is difficult to keep connected with God. We are tempted to rush our time with God. We may think, "Just tell us what to do, and stop all the talk."

Then God has a word for us, *"Be still, and know that I am God...I will be exalted in the earth"* (Ps. 46:10). Can you hear God saying, "Keep quiet and listen." Can you hear Him pleading, "Take time to get to know Me, for I am right here with you?" Do you hear the invitation, "Will you sit a while with your God?"

We will know God only as we stop long enough to read, hear and study what He has recorded in His written message to us -- the Bible. As we know and experience His divine love, our relationship with Him will be meaningful and realistic. As we spend time in His Word and get to know Him, we may even shout, "Glory belongs to our God and Father forever!" (Phil. 4:20).

*Have you struggled with spending time with God? How has this struggle affected your relationship with God?*

If we are to give honor and respect for this great and awesome God, it is imperative that we take time to recognize and understand Him. That's what this Spiritual Travel Guide is all about. If at any time we get restless and want to hurry to get it finished, please consider that there is no end to our communicating with God through studying His Word, through private meditation or through group discussion. Take time to understand Him, relate to Him and communicate with Him.

If we do not truly know Him and His love, we are not prepared to live for Him or with others in the human family and in the body of Christ. Don't be annoyed about all this theological or Bible business regarding God, because God is not a doctrine, but our loving Father. Time with our heavenly Father will enrich our lives greatly. The entire Bible provides knowledge and is talk with God, telling us how we can know Him and what He is like.


## Day 1 -- God's Nature and Qualities

Our God is a living, speaking and loving God, making Himself known to people in various ways through prophets many centuries ago, and evangelists and apostles 2000 years ago. This is all recorded in the Scriptures, which give us more than knowledge for the mind, but also faith for the heart that results in a living relationship with Him. This is a personal and intimate contact which affects and transforms our lives in order to experience God, who is a personal, eternally existent, loving and all-knowing Being (1 Tim. 1:17). He is completely beyond any earthly or human measurements. God has revealed Himself to us as the source, beginning, purpose, sustainer, power, glory and end of all things.

*1.      Describe what God is like to you at this very moment.*

**WEEK THREE**                                                   **44**

2. *Read Psalm 139:7-12. How close is God to us? How close can we be to God? How far can we get from God?*

3. *What unrealistic views and ideas about God do some people have?*

4. *What information sources have you used to develop your current understanding of who God is? Are they sources you can trust with your eternity?*

The Bible does not tell of the existence of God apart from His qualities. As we think about the character of God, we first acknowledge His holiness (Isaiah 6:3; Exodus 15:11), which means that He is perfect and *totally* separated from us sinful human beings. We pray in the Lord's Prayer, "(Hallowed) Holy be Your name." Holiness points to God's purity, radiance and moral perfection. His majesty and awesomeness are a show of His holiness. The glory of God is always associated with Jesus Christ, His Son and the world's Savior.

Consider these characteristics of God:
- God is a spirit (John 4:24).
- He is everlasting (Psalm 90:2), without beginning and without end.
- He is almighty (Gen. 17:1; Luke 1:37), so He has the power to do anything He wants to do.

- God knows everything (John 21:17). He is the architect of the universe, having perfect knowledge of His creatures and people. He knows our weaknesses, needs and the secrets of our hearts (Ps. 44:21). We are not social security numbers to God among billions of people.

- God is everywhere at the same time, omnipresent.(Jer. 23:24). There is no place that you can hide from Him. He penetrates every aspect of our life in His majestic holiness and love. This is not some vague "everywhereness," but a dynamic, gracious, real presence of our God from His Person to our person. This is shown to be an intimate connection between Jesus and us as a vine giving life to the branches (John 15:1). For example, the Holy Spirit lives in all believers in Christ, not merely figuratively through His gifts, but actually is present (1 Cor. 3:16-17).

- God is just and fair in all things (Deut. 32:4). He is the moral judge of the universe and will judge the world according to His perfect justice.

- God does not only love, but He is love (1 John 4:8). That love shows itself in that He satisfied His justice by providing the payment for sin in the death of His Son, Jesus Christ, who is the sacrificial Lamb of God.

- God is faithful (2 Tim. 2:13). He keeps His promises to us.

- He is good and compassionate (Ps. 145:9).

- God is the Ultimate Authority (Romans .13:1; 1 Peter 3:22). If we make ourselves the authority, we invite conflict, disharmony and catastrophe into our lives.

**WEEK THREE**                                                    46

His is the final authority even when He delegates control to people to be stewards over the earth (Gen. 1:28), Christian husbands to be the spiritual head of their wives (Eph. 5:22-23), parents to be obeyed by children (Eph. 6:1), and those chosen to govern to whom people are to submit. (1 Peter 2:13-14).

- God is unchanging, and His character is always the same. His truths do not change, even though human ideas may be altered regularly. His purposes for us do not change. His Son, Jesus, is the same yesterday, today, and forever. (Hebrews 13:8). "A changeless Christ for a changing world" is a strong consolation to all of God's people.

And yet in all His greatness and splendor, God cares about you. So much so that you cannot escape His presence even if you try! He wants you to experience His presence, for it always calls us back to Him.

*"Where can I go from your Spirit? Where can I flee from your presence? If I go up to the heavens, you are there; if I make my bed in the depths, you are there. If I rise on the wings of the dawn, if I settle on the far side of the sea, even there your hand will guide me, your right hand will hold me fast. If I say, 'Surely the darkness will hide me and the light become night around me,' even the darkness will not be dark to you; the night will shine like the day, for darkness is as light to you"* ( Ps. *139:7-12)*.

Everything on earth is derived from Him and dependent on Him, for He is independent and before all things. He has roots only in Himself, and everything else springs from Him. He exists by His own power, while we depend and live only by His strength. God's supreme and absolute greatness exceeds all limits, which means that He is beyond every earthly thing.  No creature or anything in the world has power over Him.

1.      *What are some of the main qualities of God named in this lesson?  Which are the most important ones to you? Why?*

2.      *How does our recognition of God's qualities and characteristics affect our personal relationship with Him and with people?*

3.      *In our daily life at home, at work, and in community affairs, how can we act so that people may think that God is insignificant?*

4.      *How can we act to show the significance and pre-eminence of God?*

While we can begin to know God through His Word, we must understand we are limited to viewing God in human images or concepts.  God is not limited in any way.  God's true character can be seen when we think of His actions, His dealings with people and His involvement in history.  We can see God guiding, loving and comforting His people in a personal relationship. We can understand that we are also His and can expect a close intimate relationship with Him, involving His actions in our life, sometimes in ways we will not fully understand.

Spend a moment in prayer now and ask God to reveal Himself to you in ways that will help you grow in your understanding of His qualities, like love, holy, etc. After your time of prayer, spend a minute in silence. Record any thoughts you might have below.

## Day 2 -- The God of Justice/Love Makes Us Right With Him

No single thought or comparison can explain God or His dealings with us in the world more than the concepts of justice and love.

God's justice, modeled in the law court, explains something of the nature of sin and salvation that no other model can illustrate. There is purity behind God's anger, too intense to ignore evil, because He is holy and righteous. He cannot pretend that wrong is not there. His justice is too true to let sin go unchecked and unpunished. God declares that the demands of His Law must be fulfilled.

At the same time, His love is too pure, lovely, gracious and absolute for Him to ignore conduct that corrupts and destroys. God can never tolerate or overlook sin. His wrath has none of the sinful associations that are attached to human anger. In the Bible, we see God's reaction to our sin and His offering of a plan to overcome it.

**WEEK THREE**<br>

*What do the following passages tell about God's justice and
love?*

| Acts 10:34 | |
|---|---|
| Romans 2:2;  5:6-11 | |
| Jeremiah 31:3 | |
| 2 Cor. 5:19 | |

The ultimate question requires an understanding of how God can be merciful and forgiving without compromising His justice. God deals justly in punishing the unjust. In His holiness, God has great love and cares about people and their sin condition.

God's justice is satisfied as He exercises His love toward sinners by giving His Son to be their Savior. By the Holy Spirit, His love brings believers to know and enjoy Him in a relationship that has made them righteous before His throne, "The righteous shall live by faith" (Romans 1:13). God's actions are ultimately designed to express His love in order to save us sinners from our own mistakes and to further His good purpose for us.

The very idea of God's wrath and judgment is naturally offensive to us. It seems barbaric and out of touch with the songs of love and peace which many in our culture sing. But the facts of justice and guilt, and absolute right and wrong still remain. Only in Christ will there be forgiveness of all wrong. Through that love, God is both just and the justifier. The burden of guilt is lifted from us and the torment of our consciences is ended by pure grace. This brings us true joy.

*How have you experienced the joy of complete forgiveness?
What thoughts have you had that rob you of this joy?*

**WEEK THREE**                                              **50**

The glory of the Gospel is that God made a way to justify us or make us right with Him. He gives this to us because of the perfect obedience and sacrifice of Christ for the guilt of our sin. It is impossible for us to deserve this grace, for grace is totally undeserved; only justice can be deserved, because we have sinned.

God does not withdraw His love from His people when our lives are not what they should be, or when we sin. That is why we can have *total confidence* in our relationship with Him, knowing that above all He wants us to be saved, to live under Him in His kingdom and to live with Him eternally.

God's love sent Jesus, His only Son, as a substitute for sinners, taking the guilt of us who could not pay the penalty for our sins. He died, the righteous for the unrighteous. Christ's death removes God's wrath against us and places it upon Christ. God's love is supreme as Christ gives us the victory.

Many Christians have been severely damaged as the result of their single-dimensional view of God. They see Him either as a God who is keeping score on their behavior or a God who is a benevolent grandfather who accepts the fact that "kids will be kids." Such slanted one-sided perceptions of God are a disaster.

It is urgent for us to know God and see Him for who He truly is, and to know Him as He has revealed Himself. The glory of God is in both His holiness/justice and His love/mercy, in which His love and kindness prevails. That's the very nature, character and being of the Almighty. Paul spoke of these two dimensions of God's glorious nature, "Consider therefore the kindness and sternness of God..."(Romans 11:22). It is necessary to see God in these two dimensions in order to pray and live right.

The key word to describe the relationship between God and people is grace, of which our loving God is always the giver, and we are always the undeserving receivers. God's grace is unmerited mercy and love seen in His forgiveness of our sins and in His goodness to us in our daily lives. Grace does not give us a rule to keep, but gives us God and the strength to live for Him.

Sin created the gulf between us and God, and our efforts cannot bridge it. The Cross of Jesus is the bridge. Faith worked by the Holy Spirit causes us to see the bridge and walk over it.

The word "justified" is borrowed from the court of law. A justified person has no legal charges against him. He is righteous or right in the eyes of the law. Because of Jesus' death on the cross, God holds no charges against us. All sin, past, present and even future, will not bring a charge against believers. We can live in the total security of a right relationship with God.

*Why should you not be afraid of God's justice?  How will you face God on Judgment Day – confident or fearful?*

Justification is the foundation upon which our right relationship with God is built totally as a gift from God. Remove the doctrine of justification, and the church has nothing to offer. Buildings stand and the traditions remain, but there is nothing left to give salvation and rehabilitation. Without being justified and having faith, church members degenerate into members of a religious club. Justification through Jesus stands totally against formal religion and idle ceremonies.

The consequence of being justified by faith is to have peace with God (Romans 5:1). This peace is based on the fact, "Therefore, there is now no condemnation for those who are in Christ" (Romans 8:1). No one can bring charges against us because Jesus has taken our own charges upon Himself.

*Why is it not arrogant to say that we will stand before God completely justified and holy?*

**WEEK THREE**

Being justified also means that we have access to God: *"Therefore, since we have been justified through faith, we have peace with God through our Lord Jesus Christ"* (Rom. 5:1). God's door is open to us, as we have been signed into the Father's presence by Jesus without any payment on our part. Our names are now written in God's family register in heaven (Luke 10:20).

1. *How do you feel about speaking boldly with all your heart, telling others that you and they are completely justified/made right with God, through the precious blood of Jesus Christ? Does the idea make you feel good or go into shock?*

2. *What would you say if someone maintained that the Godhead is one Person wearing three hats?*

3. *How would you answer a person who claims that God as the Trinity is an abstract impersonal force?*

Go to God now in prayer and ask Him to increase your understanding of justification and the impact this should have on your life. After your time of prayer, spend a minute in silence. Record any thoughts you might have below.

**WEEK THREE**                                    **53**

## Day 3 -- God the Father/Creator

The Bible teaches that there is only one God (Deut. 6:4), and in that one God are three Persons: Father, Son, and Holy Spirit (Matt. 28:19; 2 Cor. 13:14). Our faulty minds find it difficult to understand how there can be one God in whom is three Persons. Also, how each Person can be fully God and how each Person is distinct from the other two.

*What struggles have you had in believing in the Trinity, three Persons in one God? What do you think is the source of those struggles?*

Evidence of the personal nature of the Father, Son and the Holy Spirit is provided in Jesus' words in John 14-16, where He urges His disciples to believe in the Father and in Him. Here He tells of His relationship with the Father. He also tells of the Father sending the Comforter, the Holy Spirit. His followers found this difficult to understand (John 16:18). It is not surprising that we find it hard to get a clear picture of what Jesus meant. John 16:13 tells us that when the Spirit of Truth comes, He will guide us into all truth. Over the next three days, we will examine God the Father, God the Son and God the Spirit in more detail.

The doctrine of God in the Trinity is so firmly based in Scripture that it is a fundamental article of the Christian faith. He is God almighty, who has creation power, salvation power and sanctifying power. The Christian Church of all ages has confessed the Triune God in the Apostle's Creed, the Nicene Creed, and the Athanasian Creed.

Paul focuses on the Trinity and gives praise to the Three-in-One God in a Gospel explosion in Ephesians 1, which tells of God's plan of salvation for all sinners. God the Father planned it (1:3-6); Jesus Christ the Son executed God's plan (1:7-12); the Holy Spirit guaranteed that the plan would be ultimately completed (1:13-14).

**God the Father -- The Creator and Provider**

Our loving Father made us and gave us our abilities and all we need to sustain ourselves, preserving, defending, and guarding us against all evil.

*What do these verses say about God's care for us?*

| | |
|---|---|
| Gen. 9:3 | |
| Matt. 6:25 | |
| Ps. 36:6-7 | |

*What is the world's view of God? Why do many people feel that God is far away and can't be bothered?*

People who feel God is far away and uncaring have not taken the time to see what God says about Himself in the Bible.

| God created everything visible and invisible (Col. 1:16) | Created means to "make out of nothing." God spoke the word, and something was there instantaneously (Gen. 1:3). By faith, we believe that God created the world and everything in it (Ex. 20:1; Heb. 11:3). |
|---|---|
| God made us | God formed man in a special way from the dust of the ground and gave him the breath of life, making him in His own image (Gen. 1:26-27; 2:27). God also made the woman in a special way (Gen. 2:18, 21-24). Adam and Eve saw the reflection of God's holiness in themselves, for He made them in His image. |
| God provides and preserves | He preserves by natural means and miracles, and He protects by keeping evil away and making evil serve our good (Heb. 1:3; Ps. 145:15-16). |
| God created holy angels | Angels protect us (Ps. 91:10-11; Heb. 1:14). |

Doesn't it make sense that the Creator would care for the creation?

*What earthly situations most often cause us to doubt the love and care of our heavenly Father?*

Christians accept God's record of creation in Genesis by faith (Heb. 11:3). Biblical creation has its source in the One Who claims that He was the only One there. The Holy Spirit inspired the Biblical authors to write His words so that we would have an adequate basis for all we need to understand about beginnings, the

**WEEK THREE**  56

nature of our existence, and God's purpose for us.  A Biblical view consists basically of a three-fold view of history: a perfect creation, corrupted by sin, and restored by Jesus Christ.

In six days, God created everything from nothing, and each part was designed to work with all the others in perfect harmony (Gen. 1).  All this was corrupted by sin, and we no longer live in a world as God originally created it.

*Do you struggle with belief in a Biblical view of creation? Why or why not?*

Evolution is a human belief regarding the origin of everything we see in the world based on scientific theories, not evidence.  There was no other observer there, except God.  Both creation and evolution are belief systems, and *neither* can be proven scientifically.  It is a question as to whom we choose to believe: fallible people with their ever-changing theories and no credible evidence, or the infallible God with His holy and powerful nature and power.  Observations on present day situations cannot reconstruct the origin of things when no one was there to record what happened. The real issue is that there are two religions in conflict: one human and one divine, one speculation, while the other is the record of the Creator Himself.  If the account of the Bible is continually subject to reinterpretation based on the changing views of scientists, then we are left with human unproven hypotheses and flights of fancy standing before the face of the one true God.  How do you think God feels about the theory of evolution?

*"Who is this that darkens my counsel with words without knowledge?  Brace yourself like a man; I will question you, and you shall answer me. 'Where were you when I laid the earth's*

*foundation?' Tell me, if you understand" (Job 38:2-4).* God is angry with people who were not present at His creation who try to tell Him He is wrong: *"Will the one who contends with the Almighty correct Him?  Let him who accuses God answer Him!" (Job 40:2).* Those who argue against God will do well to answer the Lord as Job did, *"I am unworthy - how can I reply to You?  I put my hand over my mouth.  I spoke once, but I have no answer - twice, but I will say no more" (40:4-5).*

Whatever we believe about our origins affects our whole world view, including the purpose and the meaning of life. Christians accept God's record because they accept a God to whom they are answerable.  He is the only One who offers grace and mercy.  We are dealing with a spiritual question.  The evidence is clear to those who live by faith, "For since the creation of the world, God's invisible qualities - His eternal power and divine nature - have been clearly seen, being understood from what has been made, so that men are without excuse" (Rom. 1:20).  Christians should not stand with those who oppose God's record of creation, because, "They deliberately forget that long ago by God's Word, the heavens existed and the earth was formed out of water and by water" (2 Peter 3:5).

Removing God from creation reduces our existence to pure chance.  Is it any wonder it is so easy to devalue life if we teach people that our existence is only an accident?

We can be certain of God's creation account because Christ was there. Christ (the Word) was present.  *"In the beginning was the Word, and the Word was with God, and the Word was God.  He was with God in the beginning.  Through Him all things were made; without Him nothing was made that has been made.  In Him was life, and that life was the light of men" (John 1:1-4).*  Christ is shown to be the Lord of all creation (Col. 1:16).

**WEEK THREE**                                    

Those who tear away the fabrics of beginnings destroy the truth of their own origin and existence. The result is chaos. Genesis provides the basic account of life in the universe, the origin of human beings, of government, of sex, of marriage, of culture, of work, of nations, of death, of the Chosen people, of sin, of the Savior, of the solar system, and of diet and clothes. The understanding of all things today is dependent on their beginning.

The interrelationship of the Father with His family is the very core of the Christian faith. Christianity is the way of the Father with His family - the body of Christ. He cannot be understood by looking at earthly fathers or scientists. Christianity is not a world philosophy or wisdom but a divine-human relationship. It is not even a theology or science of God, but rather the union of God the Creator and His children.

*What does God's forming of man and woman in a special way and making them in His image mean to you for the quality of your life?*

Ask God in prayer to show you your doubt about the Trinity and God's role in creation. After your time of prayer, spend a minute in silence. Record any thoughts you might have below.

## Day 4 -- God the Son/Redeemer

The second Person of the Triune God, Jesus Christ, at one time in history, took into Himself human nature or form, fully and wholly man, but without sin (Luke 1:35).  He was conceived by the Holy Spirit and born of the virgin Mary (Matt. 1:18-25), lived, suffered, died and was resurrected, and ascended into heaven, where He sits now at the right hand of the Throne of God. Jesus Christ is the Person of the Godhead in Whom there is a union of two natures - the divine and the human clearly outlined in Col. 2:9, "In Christ all the fullness of the Deity lives in bodily form."

*What are some of the descriptions of Christ you have heard from non-Christians?*

Jesus came to earth to lay down His life for all people that they might be restored and brought back to life with God.  To accomplish this, Jesus Christ became for a period in the world's history the rejected One, the Person who bore the wrath of God against the sin of the whole human race.  As the Lamb of God, He became the slaughtered sacrifice as the payment for the guilt of all mankind.  This momentous event was planned by the Triune God and announced thousands of years prior to Jesus' arrival.  His coming in human flesh changed the course of human history. "The Lord Himself shall give you a sign: the virgin will be with child and will give birth to a son, and will call him Immanuel (God with us)" (Is. 7:14).

*Why do you believe that it was necessary for God to sacrifice His Son as a human being?  Could He not find another way to work our salvation?  Why or why not?*

**WEEK THREE**

The mission of Jesus Christ on earth was to remove the barrier that separated us from God through His death on the cross: "And are justified freely by His grace through the redemption that came by Christ Jesus" (Rom. 3:24). The cross was not the end, for three days after His death, He became alive: "...He was raised on the third day according to the Scriptures" (1 Cor. 15:4). For 40 days after His resurrection, Jesus was seen by many people on numerous occasions (Acts 1:3). Then He gave final instructions to His followers and went up into heaven where He now rules at the right hand of God (Acts 1:8-11). The results of His work to save all humanity are freely offered to us and received through faith (Eph. 2:8-9).

Jesus obeyed God's will actively and passively. In his act of obedience, Jesus lived the life of an obedient servant, totally dedicated to doing the will of His heavenly Father (2 Cor. 5:21; Gal. 4:5-6). His crucifixion was not an accident that He and the Father and the Holy Spirit had to accept. It was God's eternal plan of love for the salvation of all people. In His passive obedience, Jesus surrendered His life into death on the Cross, and so took into His own body the punishment that all sinners deserve for their sins (John 3:8; 2 Tim. 2:10; Rom. 5:19). Yet, Jesus was not a victim when He was crucified. He could have refused death, but in love, He allowed it to happen to carry out His saving mission because of His willing obedience to the Father.

***What does Jesus' death and resurrection mean to you personally today?***

The Bible also shows Jesus' condition of humiliation (stepping down from heaven to become a man, obedient to His death on the cross), and exaltation. In his state of humiliation, even though He never ceased to be God or became anything less than God, He did not fully use the power and the other divine qualities which He had as God.  Although He always possessed these attributes, He humbled Himself (Phil. 2:4-11).  In His exaltation, we see the ascended Lord (Acts 1:1-9) using His divine powers and abilities that had always been His as God (Matt. 28:19-20).  His steps into exaltation were that He descended into hell to show His victory, rose again from the dead, ascended into heaven, sits at the right hand of God the Father almighty, and from there He shall come to judge the living and the dead on the last day.

*Put this in your words:*

• *Jesus' humiliation was when:*




• *Jesus' exaltation was when:*




*What does the Bible say about Christ's work as prophet, priest and king?*

| | |
|---|---|
| **Prophet** - John 17:8 | |
| **Priest -** <br> Heb. 7:26-27, John 1:29-36 | |
| **King** – Eph. 1:20-21 Eph. 1:22, Col. 1;15-20 Rom. 14:9 | |

It is truly comforting to know that the visible Son showed us the Invisible Father   (John 1:18; 2 Cor. 4:4).   We can understand what our invisible God is like by observing the manner by which Jesus on earth dealt with people in need (Matt. 8:1-4), how boldly He confronted the devil and the demons (Mark 1:25; John 18:4-8), and how He showed love and patience to many people and was ready to sacrifice Himself (Mark 10:32-34). As Jesus treated people during His time on earth, so the Father treats us now.

No force has been able to overcome the absolute power of Christ's cross. Its influence is greater than that of any organization, university or government. Because Christ was lifted from the earth in His ascension, He draws and lifts us through the radical nature and power of the Cross. What the sun is to the solar system, what the needle is to the compass, what the heart is to the body - that the Cross is to everyone who has the hope for salvation and positive direction in life.

Jesus was not just one of the earthly saints or the greatest spirit on earth. Salvation is not found in a doctrine about Christ, but in the Person of Jesus Christ. He does not merely add something to the sum total of the world's knowledge of religion, but He is the center of all truth and life. He is the living Christ, Savior and Lord, with Whom we have a living relationship by faith.

Can you imagine a Lord ruling the world from several planks stained with blood? Jesus' Cross is His throne, which is the rallying point for all His earthly followers. The shadow of His throne stretches across the globe through the centuries: "In the Cross of Christ I glory, towering o'er the wrecks of time." A Cross, which led to the grave, also led to the open tomb and the Ascension Mount. Christianity is the only religion that sends good news from the cemetery. Jesus lives and rules!

Let every knee be bowed and every tongue confess that Jesus Christ is Lord, to the glory of God the Father! (Phil. 2:10-11).

**WEEK THREE** **63**

*1.  Has your idea of who Jesus is changed after studying this lesson? If  so, how?  What have you learned about Jesus that will change your life?*




*2.   What is your answer to a person who says that Jesus is a only moral teacher who gives us religious lessons?*




*3.   Why is Christ worthy of worship (Heb. 1:6; Phil. 2:9-11)? Of what else is He worthy (Rev. 4:11; 5:12)?*




Jesus' death and resurrection are central to your life as a Christian.  Go to God now in prayer and ask Him to show you the reality of the action God took on the Cross.  Ask God to open your eyes so that you might personally experience the victory of the Resurrection.  After your time of prayer, spend a minute in silence.  Record any thoughts you might have below.


## Day 5 -- God the Holy Spirit/Sanctifier

As the sun with its light exposes the roads which we travel with all their challenges, so the Holy Spirit penetrates the deep dark dungeons of our mind to shed light on the nature and purpose of God.  Without the sun, we have darkness like a thousand midnights.  Without the Holy Spirit, we have spiritual confusion and unbelief almost like hell itself.  Without the Spirit, we are in darkness and death.

The third Person of the Godhead is the Holy Spirit.

**What is the chief work of the Holy Spirit?**

| | |
|---|---|
| 1 Cor. 2:14;<br>1 Peter 2:9-11 | |
| 1 Cor. 6:11;<br>2 Thes. 2:13 | |
| John 16:8 | |
| John 16:13 | |
| John 16:14 | |

The work of the Holy Spirit is called regeneration (giving us new birth) and sanctification (living the Christian life).  He uses the Word as the means to invite and empower us personally to receive God's gift of salvation and sanctification (1 Peter 1:23; Rom. 10:17).  The Holy Spirit uses baptism for this new birth (John 3:6; Titus 3:5).

1.  *What does Jesus call the Holy Spirit in John 16:7?  What is the significance of this?*

2.  *How are we dependent on the work of the Holy Spirit for our salvation?  Can you take any credit for believing in Christ for salvation?  Why or why not?*

**WEEK THREE**     

The Holy Spirit does many things for us.  He enables us to respond in faith to God's love, and guarantees our eternal inheritance. (Eph. 1:13-14).  Rom. 10:14-17 teaches us that the Holy Spirit gives us the Word of God.  He enlightens our minds, persuades us and changes our minds, and empowers us to accept the Word that gives us faith to trust in Christ for salvation.  He teaches us the things that Christ wants us to do as His disciples.  He is with us at all times. *"Don't you know that you yourselves are God's temple and that God's Spirit lives in you?" (1 Cor. 3:16).*

What is the promise regarding the Holy Spirit's presence in Acts 1:8?

**God is with us, through the Spirit giving us power to do His work.  The chart below lists many of the functions and roles of the Holy Spirit.**

| | |
|---|---|
| John 14:26 | Gives us Truth |
| John 2:18-22, Acts 11:15-17 | Helps us understand the plan of God and the promise of the Father |
| John 15:26-27 Acts 4:5-14 | Gives strength for witnessing and gives us the words to say |
| Eph. 2:1 <br><br> Rom. 8:7 <br> 1 Cor. 2:14 | It is necessary for the Holy Spirit to work faith in us because we are by nature spiritually dead, enemies of God and blind so that we cannot bring ourselves to faith in Christ |
| 2 Thes. 2:13-14 | Leads us into a right relationship with Christ, reproducing Christ in us |
| John 15:8-11 1 Cor. 6:9-11 | Corrects us in order to cleanse us and convicts the world of sin |

**WEEK THREE** 66

| | |
|---|---|
| Eph. 4:10-16<br>Gal. 5:22-25 | Leads us on the path of holiness for spiritual maturity and to spiritual fruitfulness |
| Eph. 6:17<br>Eph. 6:10-17 | Protects us through spiritual weapons: the Word of God and the whole armor of God |
| Rev.5:910;<br>15:3-4<br>Acts 16:25 | Leads us to sing in unending praise even in unfavorable circum-stances |
| 1 Cor. 12:4-12<br>1 Cor. 13:1-13 | Equips us for service by giving us gifts and by providing motivation for our service and ministry |
| Acts 4:33<br>Acts 4:32ff<br>Acts 4:23-31 | Energizes us for work and gives us the power to witness by producing a fellowship, a community of caring and a fellowship for praying |
| Acts 10:19-20;<br>13:1-40<br>Acts 5:1-11 | Directs Christian mission activities and defeats the devil's schemes |
| Acts 4:32-37<br><br>Acts 12:1-17 | Teaches us to wait patiently, experience the promises of God under severe circumstances, even deprivation, prison, and death |
| Acts 2:17-18;<br>Gal. 3:28<br>Acts 2:5; 10:34;<br>11:7, 12 | Abolishes inequalities among people on the basis of sexual differences, also racial, national and cultural |
| Rom.14:15;<br>15:16<br>Rom. 7 and 8<br>Gal. 5:22-25 | Intimately involved in our moral lives to overcome the works of the flesh or sinful nature and to produce ethical behavior |
| Heb. 11:6 | Causes us to do good works. A good work is everything a believer does, speaks, or |

| John 14:15<br>1 Cor. 10:31 | thinks in faith, according to God's commands, to the glory of God for the benefit of his or her neighbor |

*How do you depend upon the Holy Spirit to meet your needs day by day? What problems do you face when you do not depend upon the work of the Holy Spirit?*

As you end your study this week, meditate on this prayer, and pray it fervently:

*Spirit of the Living God,*
*Take control of me;*
*Melt me! Mold me! Fill me! Use Me!*
*-Daniel Everson*

*How has this prayer affected your attitude? In what ways do you believe it would be a great blessing to have God melt, mold, fill and use you?*

## Major Points to Review

1. Human images or concepts limit our understanding of God's nature and qualities. How have these limits distorted your picture of God?

2. God can be described as a God of justice and a God of love. How can God be both?

**WEEK THREE**                                                      68

3. The Bible teaches there is one God and that in this God there are three persons. How does the Trinity affect your understanding of God?

4. God the Father is described as the Creator and Sustainer. How does knowing that God created all things and that He sustains them change your view of life?

5. Jesus through his action on the Cross removed the barrier that separated us from God. How does knowing you have direct access to God change your view of life?

6. God sent the Holy Spirit to live in us. What conflict has the Spirit prompted by His presence in you?

## OBSERVATIONS/REFLECTIONS ON WHAT YOU STUDIED THIS WEEK:

1. What matters or issues would you like to know more about?  What, if anything, troubled you about what you studied?


2. What new knowledge or insights have you learned?


3. How has your faith grown or been modified?


4. How will this affect your life?


**WEEK THREE** 70

# WEEK FOUR

# GOD COMMUNICATES WITH US

How can we hear from God?  God could have used a heavenly public address system or He could have talked to us individually.  But instead He chose His Word to communicate with us.  Through the Word, He forgives and changes sinful people.  The Bible conveys His message through written words.  As a result of the promises in the written Word, Baptism and Holy Communion convey the divine promise through "visible" words.

Let's review God's message to us:
- The Incarnate Word (Christ born as man)
- The written Word (Bible)
- The proclaimed Word (sermon)
- The celebrated Word (worship)
- The visible Word (Baptism and Holy Communion)
- The demonstrated Word (Christian life)

This is how God communicates to us and through us to people.

## Day 1-- God Communicates Through the Written Word

God gave us the Bible to reveal Himself, pulling back the curtain that separates us from Him.  In the Word, He tells of His relationship to all of His creation, including us.  Most importantly, He records what He has done for us and what He wants us to believe about Him and do for Him.

*How do you determine what God wants you to do for Him?*

Last week we learned a little about who God is, how He acts, why He acts the way He does, and what His plans and purposes are for all of history and for our lives.  There is much to learn from God's love letters to you.  **But what makes this book so special?**  How can we be sure it represents truth?  Have you ever wrestled with believing what the Bible says is true?

*Let's look at what the Bible says about itself.  Read the following passages and record the main message of each in the space provided.*

| | |
|---|---|
| John 17:17 | |
| 2 Peter 1:21 | |
| 1 Thes. 2:13 | |
| 2 Tim. 3:16 | |
| Job 23:12 | |
| Ps. 119:105 | |
| Jer. 23:29 | |

| John. 5:3 | |
| --- | --- |
| Rom. 1:16 | |

What an awesome thought - God spoke His thoughts to His servants. The entire content of Bible is inspired or God-breathed (2 Tim. 3:16). They recorded it for us. While it was not dictation, all the words of the Bible are God's Words because the Holy Spirit guided the writers not only in their thoughts, but even the words they wrote. The Holy Spirit Himself refuses to allow the existence of anything false or fallible. Because the Word of God is truly His words, it is a very powerful instrument that has tremendous effect on life.

*On a scale of 1-10 with 10 as the high, how would you rate the effect of the Word on your life? How?*

The Bible says, "For the Word of God is living and active. Sharper than any double-edged sword, it penetrates even to dividing soul and spirit, joints and marrow; it judges the thoughts and attitudes of the heart" (Heb. 4:12). What this means is that the Bible does not leave a single part of our life untouched, as it exposes our false beliefs. The more we read and understand the more we see how much sin is in our lives. Sometimes it can be very discouraging. But the Word doesn't stop there; it brings us forgiveness; putting us together again by the Gospel. God's Word pulsates with life. So, why do we have our Bibles closed?

*What can stop you from reading the Bible regularly?*

**WEEK FOUR** 73

Time spent in God's Word is essential. The Word alone provides the values and power for making proper decisions in moral conflicts, personal problems, human relations, and responsibilities. By the Holy Spirit, the Word will convict us with the realization that God really exists and is here, that He really cares, and that His love meets our needs and requires a response. By grace, we believers accept the Word of God because the Holy Spirit has spoken an internal word of confirmation in our hearts and minds.

*What problems or issues are you facing today about which you would like to hear from God's Word? What is the advantage of seeking answers from the  Bible versus other sources?*

Go to God now in prayer and ask Him for the strength to regularly read His Word. Pray that He might remove any barriers to your study of His Word. After your time of prayer, spend a minute in silence. Record any thoughts you might have below.

## Day 2 -- God's Message in the Old and New Testaments

Do you know what the word testament means? It means promise! So the Bible is a book of promises from God. Even though it was written over the span of more than a thousand years by over 40 different authors it still fits together perfectly, telling the great plan God has for all people, including you!

*Why do you think there are two parts to the Bible?*

The Bible is divided into the news of the Old Testament (before the birth of Christ) and the New Testament (after the birth of Christ). The Old Testament is the history of the creation of the world, the fall of mankind and the promises of God to save His creation. The major subject of most of the Old Testament is the Israelites. God chose Israel as the nation from which He brought forth a Savior, Jesus Christ. We can learn a lot about God by studying the ways in which He deals with the Israelites.

The New Testament gives us a record of the earthly life, suffering, death and resurrection of Jesus Christ, together with the account of the spread of the Gospel through the Christian Church. In the New Testament we see the fulfillment of God's promise to all people -- to save them from sin and death. This is the main message of the Old and New Testament -- God's action to save us. What could be more natural, a Creator setting out to save His creation, which had gone astray?

*Have you ever questioned the reliability of the Bible? Why or why not?*

From the very first book of the Bible we can see God's grace or love for us, His creation. Because of the sin of Adam and Eve we have been removed from the presence of our Creator. The whole Bible tells of God's plan to get us back, not through our good works, but by His love, His grace.

*How would you describe the concept of grace?*

**WEEK FOUR**                                    75

We see God's attitude toward us, His creation, unfold in the Word. From cover to cover we can find one consistent message of His love for us and desire for us to be His children. God's grace is favor or kindness shown to us without regard to our worth or merit and in spite of what we deserve.

*As you look at your life so far, what do you think you deserve from God? Why do you deserve this?*

As a Christian, you will spend the rest of your life studying the greatest truth in the world. Simply stated this truth says we don't get what we deserve from God. Instead of God's anger and wrath, we get His forgiveness and love, not because of what we have done, but because of what God has done for us through His Son, Jesus.

The graph below gives you an outline for the whole Bible. Review each of the major sections listed below. Look at your Bible. Does it have any study notes at the beginning of each chapter? On each page? It is important to get a good study Bible so you can explore and experience God's great grace and His plan for you!

| Old Testament | |
| --- | --- |
| **5 books of Moses** | |
| Genesis, Exodus, Leviticus, Numbers, Deuteronomy | An account of the origin of the universe and the human race, telling of the children of Israel's obedience and disobedience, bondage and deliverance, and their pilgrimage and 40 years wandering in the wilderness. Laws concerning morals, cleanliness, food, and sacrifices to have access to God. |

| 12 historical books | |
| --- | --- |
| Joshua, Judges, Ruth, 1 & 2 Samuel, 1 & 2 Kings, 1 Chronicles, 2 Chronicles, Ezra, Nehemiah, Esther | Conquest of Canaan under Joshua, and the division of the land among the 12 tribes. Six times Israel was conquered and delivered through 15 judges. There is the history of Ruth, Samuel, Saul, David, Elijah and Elisha. An account is given of the return of the Jews from captivity, of the rebuilding of the temple and the walls of Jerusalem, and of the re-establishment of sacred ordinances. |
| **5 poetic books** | |
| Job | Tells of Job's problems and his patience under afflictions |
| Psalms | Collection of 150 spiritual songs, poems and prayers used through the centuries by Old Testament believers for worship and devotions, many authored by David. They are the "heart language of God." |
| Proverbs | Proverbs is a collection of moral and religious rules and discourses. |
| Ecclesiastes | Solomon's wisdom on the paths in life that lead to emptiness. |
| Song of Songs | Solomon's wedding song honoring marriage and the physical relationship between man and wife. |
| **5 major Prophets** | |
| Isaiah | A book of messianic and salvation prophecies |
| Jeremiah & Lamentations | Jeremiah takes us up to the Captivity, telling of backsliding, bondage and restoration of the Jews - repeated in Lamentations. |
| Ezekiel | Ezekiel poetically portrays the sad condition |

**WEEK FOUR**

| | |
|---|---|
| | of God's people and the way to gain future glory. |
| Daniel | Daniel is a personal biography with prophetic visions concerning events in both secular and sacred history. |
| **12 minor Prophets** | |
| Hosea | Shows the sins and apostasy of Israel, named spiritual adultery. |
| Joel | Urges repentance as "the Day of Lord" is a time of blessing. |
| Amos | Denounces selfishness through a series of visions. |
| Obadiah; Jonah | The "reluctant" missionary learned the lesson of obedience and divine mercy after he rejected God's will. |
| Micah; Nahum; Habakkuk | Written in the Babylonian period, shows why a just God providentially can allow a wicked nation to oppress Israel. |
| Zephaniah | Through threatenings, relates a vision of the future glory of Israel. |
| Haggai | Scolds the people for slowness in building the second temple, promising a return of God's glory. |
| Zechariah; Malachi | A graphic picture of the closing history of the Old Testament, showing the necessity of reform before the coming of the Messiah. |
| **New Testament** | |
| **Gospels** | |
| Matthew | One of the 12 apostles, stresses the kingdom of Christ, showing Jesus to be the kingly Messiah of Jewish prophecy. |
| Mark | Emphasizes the supernatural power of Jesus |

| | and His acts over nature, disease, and demons. |
| --- | --- |
| Luke | The "beloved physician," presents the most complete biography of Jesus, portraying Him as the Son of Man, full of compassion. |
| John | The "beloved disciple," reveals Jesus as the Son of God and records His deeper teachings. |
| **Historical** | |
| Acts | Luke writes a sequel to his Gospel with the theme being the origin and growth of the early Church, from the ascension of Christ to the imprisonment of Paul in Rome. |
| **Paul's 13 letters written to congregations in various cities, to pastors and to individual Christians** | |
| Romans | A masterful exposition of Law and Gospel, and shows the plan of salvation, offering exhortations related to spiritual, social and civic duties. |
| 1 Corinthians | Tells of the cleansing of the Church from various evils, and presents doctrinal instructions. |
| 2 Corinthians | Characterizes Paul's view of the pastoral ministry. |
| Galatians | The doctrine of justification by faith with warnings against false teachers and reverting back to the Law |
| Ephesians | The glorious plan of salvation and the high purpose of Christians and the Church. |
| Philippians | Reveals Paul's intense devotion to Christ, his joyful experience in prison, and his deep concern that the Church should be steadfast |

| | in sound doctrine. |
| --- | --- |
| Colossians | The all-embracing glory of Christ as the Head of the Church, calling for abandoning of all worldly philosophy and sin. |
| 1Thessa-lonians | Offers exhortations, and the comfort and hope of the final coming of Christ. |
| 2Thessa-lonians | Enlarges on above. |
| 1 Timothy & 2 Timothy | Provides counsel to the young pastor as his "true son in the faith," concerning his conduct in ministerial work. |
| Titus | Gives exhortation to a trusted pastor friend in a difficult place, emphasizing especially the doctrine of good works. |
| Philemon | Urges his former owner to receive and forgive Onesimus, a runaway slave. |
| **8 general letters** | |
| Hebrews | Tells of the great glory of Christ and of the blessings of the new dispensation, which is compared with those of the Old Testament. |
| James | Emphasizes practical faith as seen in good works. |
| 1 Peter; 2 Peter | The first letter encourages scattered and separated Christians to follow the example of Jesus and live victorious and holy lives, while his second letter is a warning against false teachers. |
| 1 John, 2 John, 3 John | Presents a deep spiritual message to different kinds of believers in the church, who have fellowship and brotherly love, also stresses divine truth against worldly error, warning |

| | against heresy and false teachers. |
|---|---|
| Jude | Provides historic examples of apostasy and divine judgment, warning against immoral teachers. |
| Prophecy of John | |
| Revelation | This is a series of prophetic visions portraying a great moral conflict between divine and satanic powers, ending in the victory of the Lamb, Jesus Christ. |

Your Bible is one of the most important investments you can make. Go to a Christian bookstore and look at all the Bibles currently available. Study carefully a copy of "GOD'S WORD" (WORLD PUBLISHING, Grand Rapids, MI 49418) which is an easy to read, accurate translation of the Bible – look also at the Student's Edition. **Give your evaluation of the "GOD'S WORD" Bible to your facilitator or study group. Besides "GOD'S WORD," record the names of a few of the Bibles that appeal to you most and why you like them.**

Go to your Father now in prayer. Thank Him for the gift of His Word. Ask Him to open your mind to the Word. After your time of prayer, spend a minute in silence. Record any thoughts you might have below.

## Day 3 -- God's Message of Law and Gospel

The two main teachings or doctrines in the Bible are Law and Gospel. The Law informs us of many things that we are to do and not to do. It shows us we have sinned and are condemned.

*Review the following passages and record how they speak to you:*

| | |
|---|---|
| Rom. 3:20 | |
| Deut. 27:26 | |
| Ex. 34:11 | |
| Deut. 5:11 | |

The Law is designed by God to convict us of our sin. The Law has three functions, acting as:
- a mirror to show our sins,
- a curb to discourage and stop sinful actions,
- a guide to show the will of God for our lives.

The Gospel on the other hand:
- shows us our Savior from sin,
- reveals what God has done and still does for our salvation,
- gives strength for Christian living.

**Compare the Law and Gospel in the way they affect and influence us:**

<table>
<tr><td>

*LAW*

Bad News
We are lost
Destroys
Self-righteous
Works on behavior

Makes people sad, mad
Condemned by God's justice
Freezes the heart
Weight is on man
Puts us on our own-(do something)

Obedience to commands
Multiplies sin
Keeps in slavery
Leads to death

</td><td>

*GOSPEL*

Good News
We are found
Heals
Christ-righteous
Works on the heart
That directs behavior
Makes people glad
Saved by God's grace
Thaws the heart
Weight is on God
Puts us in Christ-
(faith)

Faith in promises
Erases sin
Makes us free
Leads to life

</td></tr>
</table>

The Law and Gospel are to be used with all people. However, the Law is to be presented especially to unrepentant sinners, and the Gospel especially to those who are repentant and especially troubled because of their sins.

*What does the word repentant mean to you? In which categories shown above do you most often find yourself?*

Believers do not gain assurance of salvation by keeping the Law, but by embracing God's mercy in Christ. The requirements of the Law have been fully met for the Christian by Christ's obedience, suffering, death and resurrection. The Law for the Christian is still an expression of the will of God in the sense of being a guide.  A response to God's love is to seek to be obedient to the Law by the power of the Holy Spirit to glorify Christ.

When we are self-satisfied or arrogant, we need to hear the Law as the Word of judgment and condemnation from God. When we hear this, it points us to the only possible solution, Jesus Christ.  When we are in agony because of our sin, we need to hear the promise of God's mercy through Christ given in the Gospel, which then sends us back to the Law as a guide for righteous living.  The Ten Commandments given to the Israelites (God's chosen people) are a moral form or code of the Law of God for Christians.

Most importantly, only the Gospel of Christ's love gives us the power and motivation to obey the Law, even though only partially.  We are justified by faith for doing good works (Eph. 2:8-10). The Gospel sets us free to obey God.  It releases us from legalisms and moralisms which say, "Here is a rule.  Keep it." Grace says, "Here is God, be like Him!", and also gives strength through the Holy Spirit to work at it.

Both Law and Gospel have their source in God and Divine Revelation, and their tension is resolved in Jesus Christ. This cannot be understood by reason, but only grasped by faith. Martin Luther said the Law differs from the Gospel just as a demand or threat differs from a gift.

The unity of Law-Gospel is seen as the Law drives us to the Gospel, and the Gospel through forgiveness points Christians to the Law for guidance for life. The Law points us to the Gospel so we may be made righteous, while the Gospel sends us to the Law to inquire what God's will is.  The Gospel without Law becomes cheap grace, while the Law without the Gospel becomes work-righteousness.

1.  *In your own words, describe the Law.*

**WEEK FOUR**                                                  **84**

*2. In your own words, describe the Gospel.*

When we discover from the Law that it was our sins that sent Jesus to the Cross, then the Gospel moves us to repentance and faith. True repentance does not result from a fear of God's wrath or punishment, but from a Gospel awareness of God's love and forgiveness in Christ.

*Why are the Law and Gospel the important factor for shaping and maintaining a strong spiritual life?*

Growing in your understanding of the differences between Law and Gospel will strengthen your faith. Ask God in prayer to show you how to distinguish between Law and Gospel. After your time of prayer, spend a minute in silence. Record any thoughts you might have below.

## Day 4 -- The Good News of Salvation

History records a few times when a man volunteered to be a substitute for a soldier who was called to military service by a government, and then the substitute died in battle. Jesus was called by God to be a perfect substitute for sinful people - all of us - to make us free from the eternal death we should have experienced. That is the Good News, which we summarize here.

*Why can we not save ourselves from our sins?*

Christ's sacrifice and redemption becomes ours by grace through faith. God gives us the gift of faith. for faith is impossible by our human nature because we are dead in sin and enemies of God. Only by the work of the Holy Spirit are we able to have a saving faith.

Jesus' perfect sacrificial death set us free from: 1) sin, as He took our guilt on Himself, suffered the punishment we deserved, and freed us from the power of sin; 2) death, for He was punished with the death we deserve, freed us from the fear of dying as He took away the power of eternal death, and defeated death by rising again; 3) the devil, as He overcame all the temptations of Satan and conquered him by taking away Satan's power to accuse us and control our lives.

Jesus died for the whole world, as He paid the price to save all people from their sins, no one excluded. All this was done for you and me individually. Jesus' resurrection makes our faith sure. For many people .this seems too simple. As a result, they never experience the freedom of faith. They wrongly assume if it's free and they don't have to do anything, it can't be true.

*How does doubt try to steal your faith?*



Jesus' action on the Cross has left us fully and freely forgiven. This salvation is presented most clearly in John 3:16, "For God so loved the world, that He gave His one and only Son, that whoever believes in Him shall not perish but have eternal life." God does not just say that He loves all people, but He proves it by His unconditional love and by sacrificing Jesus, His only Son, in our place. Separation from Him was ended, and now a loving relationship with God was restored. As our substitute,

**WEEK FOUR**

Christ made satisfaction (atoned) for our sins by paying the penalty of our guilt (2 Cor. 5:21; Is. 53:4-5). What our substitute, Christ, did for us is credited to us. Our sins were charged to Christ, and His righteousness was given to us.

Salvation or justification by faith is the central teaching of the Christian faith. Anyone who tries to add requirements to our salvation is not speaking the truth of the Bible. What great news this is!

*Why will we not properly understand the other parts of the Bible (especially the Law parts) if we do not understand that we are saved by grace only through faith by the Holy Spirit?*

Salvation is yours! Enjoy it as you live for God. Ask God in prayer to impress deeply on your heart the certainty of your salvation. Thank Him for the gift of Jesus. After your time of prayer, spend a minute in silence. Record any thoughts you might have below.

**Day 5 -- The Bible as Information/Spiritual Formation**

A big problem for the Christian is to look at the Bible mainly as a source of information or doctrines about God. Every Christian is tempted to stop with head knowledge or allow faith to stay in the mind as an intellectual exercise. Therefore, some Christians see no need for studying God's Word because they heard and learned it when they first became Christians or joined the church.  However, there is another major purpose of God's Word - spiritual formation or transformation.

The Bible is more than doctrines about God.  It is a life-changing message.  Many people are afraid of this change, finding it difficult to take the first steps.  Remember God's plan for your life will be revealed through these changes.  It is a joy- filled journey that will lead you to the true source of happiness and contentment. This is a road overflowing with the satisfaction of knowing a loving, caring God who is concerned about every detail of your life.

*What do the following Scripture passages say about the impact of God's Word on a person's life?*

| | |
|---|---|
| Titus 1:16 | |
| Titus 2:14 | |
| Titus 3:8 | |

Biblical knowledge provides benefits related to reality and faith, brings values for our decisions, gives stability during testing and temptation, equips us to handle the truth correctly and to detect error, and gives us confidence for our daily lives.

Spiritual formation, the inner development of character in a believer, is a major purpose of Bible study.  Spiritual formation is the process of being formed in the image of Christ.  It is moving from knowing to being to doing.  It involves informing the mind, and forming the life.  One of the vital dynamics of Christianity is to be formed spiritually in every action, in every response, and in

**WEEK FOUR**                                                     88

every relationship.  The result is believers who are ready to act to carry out the mission of reaching others with the Gospel.

Spiritual formation involves our receiving the Word.  We can sense this activity in the following ways:

1. In our minds -- God enlightens our minds through His Word to perceive Him and get meaning for our lives.

2. In our will -- God touches our will (hearts) by inspiring us with assurance, hope, and the willingness and strength needed to serve, despite our weakness.

3. Through our emotion -- God reaches us through our emotions or feelings by the Gospel, which is His gentle touch of loving care and power.

4. By our imagination --  we receive the impulse of God's grace in our imagination.  This does not mean we are making it up.  God uses His Holy Spirit helps us visualize what God wants us to do.

5. Through our memory -- The memory is another channel of human reception as God stimulates our stored memory to recall His Word and experiences of His love, especially to prevent us from repeating previous mistakes.

*Why are some Christians more interested in doctrinal knowledge than in experiencing spiritual formation?*

Questions of information lead us to ask, "What are the facts?"  Spiritual formation raises the question, "To what is this leading us?  What should we be and do?"  As we grow and change into the people that God desires us to be, we will experience great joy, contentment and purpose.

**WEEK FOUR**                                         89

Reading and studying the Bible consistently and systematically allows God to direct us into all truth and daily practice. Other Christians, especially those in your small group, will encourage you to act on what you are learning. Are you ready for more practice of your faith?

*"Therefore, I urge you, brothers, in view of God's mercy, to offer your bodies as living sacrifices, holy and pleasing to God-- this is your spiritual act of worship. Do not conform any longer to the pattern of this world, but be transformed by the renewing of your mind. Then you will be able to test and approve what God's will is-- his good, pleasing and perfect will (Rom. 12:1-2).*

Unfortunately, we have mental, attitudinal and behavioral barriers in our personal habits which inhibit or even stop us from being transformed in the sense of Rom. 12:1-2. We need constant encouragement from the Word and those around us to continue on this path or journey of transformation. As we are transformed, we gain the strength and maturity to deal with life and death in full confidence. It is God's plan for us to experience His freedom in all circumstances!

Ask God in prayer to let the Word change you. Ask Him to remove the fears and insecurities that might hold you back. After your time of prayer, spend a minute in silence. Record any thoughts you might have below.

## Major Points to Review

1. On what points do you struggle in accepting the authority of God's plan as presented in the Bible?

2. The Bible is divided into Law and Gospel. How does this distinction affect your understanding of the Bible?

3. Describe Christ's action on the Cross, and what it means for you.

4. The Bible has been given to us for our transformation. What are the difficulties of life transformation for you? How can these difficulties be overcome?

## OBSERVATIONS/REFLECTIONS ON WHAT YOU STUDIED THIS WEEK:

1. What matters or issues would you like to know more about? What, if anything, troubled you about what you studied?

2. What new knowledge or insights have you learned?

3. How has your faith grown or been modified?

4. How will this affect your life?

**WEEK FOUR**                                    

# WEEK FIVE

# GOD GIVES US HIS SPECIAL RICHES

Part of God's plan in the Word is for us to experience His love and grace in special ways. Baptism and Communion are sacred acts or sacraments which Christ established or commanded Christians to do. Jesus directs us to use very common everyday things in the sacraments; water, wine and bread. These physical elements are coupled with the supernatural power of God's Word so that we might experience God's grace. We cannot fully explain how these sacred acts work. By faith we are obedient to God's commands which assure that through them, He offers, gives and seals to us forgiveness of sin, eternal life and salvation.

God's Word also directs us to a life of worship. Worship is an opportunity for us to receive and respond to God's Word. Times of worship may include the pure Gospel of baptism and communion. The more of His Word we understand, the more awesome God becomes and the more we desire to worship Him. Unfortunately, many people do not experience the joy of worship because they have not yet fully understood the greatness of the gift of God's love.

## Day 1-- Baptism, Its Nature and Benefits -- God Gives New Life

Have you ever wished you could start over? Sometimes when we examine all the mistakes and sin in our lives, it seems almost hopeless. Fortunately, because of the process of spiritual rebirth, our lives are not hopeless. As Christians, we get the chance to start over every day. We can know this promise very clearly in our baptism by the complete forgiveness of our mistakes.  Remembering our baptism every day gives us a fresh start - a clean slate because through our baptism God claims us as His forgiven children.  Once again, we are touched with the undeserved gift of God's grace.

Baptism is a spiritual rebirth.  As a result of Adam and Eve's original sin, we are born spiritually corrupt and evil. Through baptism, we are reborn.

*What does Romans 7:18 say about what lives in us?*




*How would you describe our new selves through baptism according to Ephesians 4:24?*




Many people get confused about the nature and purpose of baptism.  Some say it is done as a sign that you are already a Christian.  But is that all it is?

Baptism is initiated as God's action, not ours.  He calls, and we are to respond.  He offers, and we receive.  He commands, and we are to obey. Our new birth (regeneration) is not something we do.  It is something God does for us.  We see baptism as the beginning of God's action of grace and love in our lives.  Because baptism is God's initiative it is pure Gospel - God's loving action toward undeserving and helpless, sinful human beings.  Baptism is a real event of God's mercy, power and presence, commanded by Him.

Through baptism, we experience God making us into new spiritual people.  We sometimes call this regeneration. This washing of regeneration joins us with Christ and places us into God's family. It is His means of uniting us with Him and to each other.

*Read each of the following passages and make a brief note for each regarding the need for baptism and benefits of baptism:*

| The Need for Baptism | |
| --- | --- |
| Rom. 5:12 | |
| Ps. 51:5 | |
| Matt. 28:18-19 | |
| **The Nature and Benefits of Baptism** | |
| 1 Cor. 6:11 | |
| Titus 3:5 | |
| 1 Cor. 12:13 | |
| Gal. 3:27 | |
| Rom. 6:3-5 | |
| Col. 2:12 | |

**WEEK FIVE**

| Acts 22:16 | |
|---|---|
| 1 Peter 3:21 | |

At our baptism, we receive the Holy Spirit, not in a first installment, but in full measure, and no further baptism is required or is beneficial. As we grow up in our faith, the Spirit continues His saving work in us, leading us away from sin and towards the new life God has for us.

The original Greek word "baptize" means to use water in various ways: immerse, wash, pour, or sprinkle. The amount of water does not make baptism more or less valid. The Word of God is the power, and the water is the element or instrument in baptism. The water is the instrument, while the spoken Word is the power that performs the miracle of new birth and gives saving faith.

***With what you now know about baptism, when do you think a person should be baptized?***

God's grace through baptism is the only revealed answer in the Word for children's salvation. It is the only way children can become or be members of the body of Christ, or else their guilt remains before God. If they are not baptized, they are not part of the body of Christ (1 Cor. 12:13). This is the only way that children are no longer condemned in their sinful flesh, but receive the spiritual blessing of receiving the Spirit of God (John 3:5-6).

**WEEK FIVE**

*"But if anyone causes one of these little ones who believe in me to sin, it would be better for him to have a large millstone hung around his neck and to be drowned in the depths of the sea"* (Matt. 18:6).

From this verse, we see that children do indeed sin. If you are a parent, you have seen examples of this sin from the earliest days of your child's life. God wants to extend His gift of grace to babies. He makes it clear that the sacred act of baptism is valid for children: "Repent and be baptized, every one of you in the name of Jesus Christ for the forgiveness of your sins...the promise is for you and your children..." (Acts 2:38-39).

Col. 2:11-12 reminds us that circumcision performed on Israelite boys in the Old Testament has a similarity to baptism, but baptism is the circumcision of the heart. Babies in Israel did not make the decision to be circumcised, nor were they really conscious of what was happening. The parents acted on the command and promise of God.

The proposal of "adults only" baptism was introduced as a practice in a few churches about 500 years ago. There has been no time in history when infant baptism has not been practiced, having been done at Christ's time. Questions or doubts are human arguments and they can never outweigh Christ's Great Commission to baptize all nations, including infants. Some people would have us wait until an "age of accountability" somewhere around the age of 12 to baptize children. The Bible makes no mention of an "age of accountability" or automatic salvation until the age of 12. Such human opinion rejects God's justice and limits His love on the basis of human reason. The baby's entrance into the world is by physical birth, so its entrance into the kingdom of Christ is by spiritual birth by water and the Spirit (baptism).

**WEEK FIVE**

Baptism spiritually means everything that water means physically: cleansing and health. We are saved by grace through faith, which is mediated by baptism. Baptism is a method God uses to dispense that grace. Without grace, no person, not even a baby, can stand before the Judgment Seat of God justified and declared righteous.

Ask God in prayer to strengthen your understanding of His plan for people through baptism. After your time of prayer, spend a minute in silence. Record any thoughts you might have below.

## Day 2 -- Baptism -- Its Power for Life and Growth

Baptism is a tremendous power that enables Christians to grow in faith. Throughout our lives, baptism assures us that we belong to God. God made us His own. We have rejected the devil and his evil ways. We have promised to live for and serve Christ. Baptism gives power which helps us in the struggle to live as children of God.

Baptism offers you great strength and encouragement for daily living when your old self is very active, you are tempted, or you fall into sin; also when you doubt God's love, or you face worries and problems. Your baptism makes you sure that you have been set free from the slavery of sin to be servant of God. You can look forward to living forever with God as an heir in hope of eternal life.

*Describe a temptation that you face regularly. The next time think about your baptism as the temptation occurs. Record the results below.*

**WEEK FIVE**                                              97

Because we are baptized, the Holy Spirit works in us to lead us to daily repentance.  When we repent, it is just as if the old sinful self is pushed back into the water of baptism and drowned all over again.  When we repent, the new self takes control again by the Holy Spirit, and we will want to love and serve our heavenly Father.  This cycle of repentance, forgiveness and reconciliation with our Father is always available to us.  No sin is too big or too persistent for God!

Unfortunately, some people treat baptism superstitiously as though it were magic.  They think it is an automatic passport to heaven, wrongly believing that when baptism occurs, heaven is guaranteed.  The problem is that as we grow up it is possible to reject the Holy Spirit's work in our lives.  We see this illustrated in the parable of the soils told by Jesus.

*"The one who received the seed that fell among the thorns is the man who hears the word, but the worries of this life and the deceitfulness of wealth choke it, making it unfruitful"* (Matt. 13:22).

The heart of baptism is the word of promise with its power.  Only faith can receive such a promise.  Such faith is the gift of the Holy Spirit and a miracle of grace.

Baptism reminds us of our need to die to sin and arise to holy service to God, keeping God's work in us from becoming unfruitful.  There are no shortcuts or substitutes for this daily dying so that we may be alive to God.  Our baptism is a power to salvation, and a power that motivates us to use our lives in accordance with His will.  We will spend the rest of our lives on this journey of becoming more like Him.  Fortunately for us, God's action in baptism provides  spiritual power for our journey.

Ask God in prayer to strengthen you to live in the power of your baptism.  Thank Him for this gift and the power it brings

**WEEK FIVE**

to your life. After your time of prayer, spend a minute in silence. Record any thoughts you might have below.


## Day 3 -- Invited to the Feast -- The Lord's Supper

Another source of strengthening against sin is the Lord's Supper. This is not just a feast, but THE FEAST - Jesus coming to give us His body and blood in, with and under the bread and wine. God offers us great gifts in this communion with Him at His Table.

*Describe your present understanding of communion:*


Immediately before His betrayal on Thursday of Holy Week, Jesus met with His disciples in an upper room in Jerusalem to celebrate the Passover meal (Luke 22:19-20). Passover is a Jewish celebration of their release from captivity as slaves in Egypt. Jesus would soon free all people from the slavery of sin by His death on the cross.

*How does the Lord's Supper set you free?*


Jesus replaced that Passover with a new and better Meal, which He commanded His disciples to celebrate often in remembrance of Him (Matt. 26:26-29). Jesus knows that we need to be strengthened in our understanding of His love for us. Holy

**WEEK FIVE**                                        **99**

Communion is designed just for that purpose, to grow in our understanding of our forgiveness through Jesus.

*"This is my blood of the covenant, which is poured out for many for the forgiveness of sins" (Matt. 26:28)*

In the Lord's Supper, we eat and drink bread and wine, which have been consecrated by the words of Christ's institution. Consecration is the act of setting apart, or dedicating, something for God's use.

In, with and under the bread and wine we receive with our mouths, but in a manner which we cannot explain or understand, the true Body and Blood of Christ (real presence). Christians are to celebrate this sacrament often in remembrance of Jesus, celebrating our freedom from the slavery of sin. Other names for this holy meal are the Sacrament of the Altar, the Lord's Table, and the Eucharist.

We firmly believe in the real presence of Christ's body and blood in the Lord's Supper because Jesus says, "This is My body, which was given for you." "This cup is the new covenant of my blood, which is poured out for you." The bread and wine are not changed into the body and blood of Christ as some faiths believe, for the Bible expressly declares that we eat bread and drink wine in this sacrament. (1 Cor. 11:26).

***Have you struggled with understanding the presence of Christ in communion? Why or why not?***

It should not surprise us that Jesus is present in the elements of communion. After all, Jesus promises that, "...where two or three come together in my name, there am I with them"

(Matt. 18:20).  If we believe this, it should not be to difficult to accept the real presence of Christ in the bread and wine.

We should receive the Lord's Supper frequently because Christ commands us to do so.  You might ask, "Why should we go to Communion when we already have forgiveness, life and salvation through baptism and the Word?"  We approach the Lord's Table to be strengthened in our faith and the forgiveness of our sins through our Lord Jesus Christ.  This results in strength for Christian living, remembrance of Christ and His great suffering and death for us, confession of the crucified Christ before all people, and witness that we are of one faith and united spiritually with those who commune with us. Even when we feel unworthy, God can come to us through Communion and reassure us of His love for us.

We prepare ourselves to receive Holy Communion in a worthy way by examining ourselves beforehand.

***What are we to do before taking Holy Communion according to 1 Cor. 11:27-29?  How could you take Communion in an unworthy manner?***

This is a feast of remembrance, for we recall Jesus giving Himself for us as the perfect sacrifice. The Lord's Supper takes us back to the cross of Calvary.  We remember our Lord's victory over sin, death and the devil -- and celebrate it.  We remember our promised share in the great victory feast in heaven -- and look forward to it.

The invited guests of this wonderful feast are people who know they are sinners needing God's grace and forgiveness, who repent, who believe the body and blood of Jesus are truly present, who believe that Jesus here gives forgiveness.  This is the family of God, God's people, joined in fellowship with Christ and with one another.  This feast is a "communion," a coming together in faith as one.

Faith makes us ready for the sacrament. When you trust that Jesus' invitation is for you, an unworthy sinner, and you believe Jesus' words that He gave His body and blood for the forgiveness of your sins, God Himself has made you ready. The Holy Spirit helps you to examine yourself, to confess your sins, and to want God's gifts in this sacred meal.  You cannot make yourself ready by trying to be good enough to deserve God's gifts.

You will know you are ready for communion when you answer yes to these questions:

- Am I really sorry for my sins?
- Do I really believe that Jesus died for me and that He gives me His body and blood in the sacrament for the forgiveness of sins?
- Do I honestly intend with God's help to fight against sin and to live as God's child?

In your prayer time today, ask God for a proper understanding of the Lord's Supper so that it will strengthen you to battle sin and evil.  After your time of prayer, spend a minute in silence.  Record any thoughts you might have below.

## Day 4 -- Living With God Through Worship

Many think of worship as something that happens only in church on Sunday.  But worship is not limited to special times and places.  Worship is a way of life.  Our whole life as Christians is worship -- either of God or in a negative sense worshipping idols of our own making.

**WEEK FIVE**                                              102

*"Jesus said to him, "Away from me, Satan! For it is written: 'Worship the Lord your God, and serve him only" (Matt. 4:10).*

We worship God because He is worth so much to us. He is worthy of our praise, honor, love and obedience. He is great and awesome, as we studied during the third week. He created us, saved us, gave us faith and made us His own through baptism. We worship Him because of all He has done for us.

***Describe the ways in which you currently worship God.***

We have many opportunities to worship. We can worship privately during our prayers and devotions. Families can worship together. Your small group also worships together. We worship together as a congregation celebrating the sacraments, and listening to God's Word in preaching and in songs. In all worship we respond to God with our hearts, believing in Him and adoring Him with our words by praising and thanking Him, and with our lives by being faithful and obedient to Him.

We cannot equate worship with merely "going to church." Having been baptized into the family of God, we Christians are to gather together regularly for worship and praise. It is a celebration of God's supreme worth, as His "worthiness" is extolled. We come to God with a sense of His holiness and awesomeness -- His worth.

***How do you understand God's worth to you at this moment?***

Many times, it is difficult to understand the worth of God because of the other things in our lives we place ahead of God.

**WEEK FIVE**

Yet, none of these things can save us.  Our worship is directed at One who is the source of our lives. Worship results from truly knowing God, His mercy and love.  We worship God because of who He is and what He has done for us, and because of the loving relationship we have with Him.

The focus of worship is away from ourselves, and placed on God.  This worship should be built into every part of our lives day by day.  Rich intake of God's Word, especially together with other believers, will make worship an informal daily experience rather than only a formal weekly affair.

*The Bible speaks of many expressions of worship. Examine each of the passages below and briefly note what you learn about worship.*

| Worship | |
|---|---|
| 2 Chron. 5:13 | |
| Eph. 5:19 | |
| Ps. 46:10 | |
| Ps. 95:6 | |
| Ps. 85:6 | |
| Ps. 63:4 | |
| Ps. 96:9 | |

**WEEK FIVE** 

| Ps. 122:1 | |
|---|---|
| Ps. 134:1 | |
| 2 Chron. 7:6 | |
| Luke 2:14 | |
| Ps. 150 | |
| John 4:24 | |
| 1 Chron. 25:1 | |

True worship must always be directed toward the Living God. It is not a performance in order to display the talents of pastors, singers, or anyone else. The focus must be on fellowship with God.

God forbids us to treat anyone or anything as our God instead of Him or beside Him. Strictly speaking, there are no "other gods" beside the Triune God (Is. 45:5), but there are many things which people throughout the world regard and worship as God (1 Cor. 8:4-6). Sometimes these are in the context of other religions, like Hinduism or Buddhism. Other times, gods are just the things of this world we put before God. The true God is to be worshipped exclusively (Matt. 4:10). People have other gods when they regard and worship any creature as God, when they believe in a god who is not the Triune God (John 5:23), and when they fear, love or trust in any person or being as they should in God alone (Matt.10:37; Prov. 3:5).

*If you struggle with worshipping something other than God, stop for a moment and take this matter to God. Ask Him to help you focus on Him and Him alone. Write your prayer below.*




Our worship is false when we love others more than God, love good living, money and the pleasures of the world, and when we trust in our own strength and in other people.

Healthy worship is a product of healthy belief and healthy learning. The Word in our hearts will express itself in worship on our lips. A living God should receive lively praise from His people. Worship, both public and private, should be so meaningful that we regret that it is over and are always ready to return to it.

While our whole life is worship, it is important to set aside special times to worship. We worship God through personal devotions for private meditation, family worship, small group worship and congregational worship. It is a great opportunity to listen and speak to God. When we stop focusing on ourselves, and look to God and see all the good things that He has done, our mouths and lives will express praise and thanksgiving. (Ps. 106:1).

Go back and read the prayer you wrote above. Ask God again for a pure heart so that you might worship only Him. After your time of prayer, spend a minute in silence. Record any thoughts you might have below.


**WEEK FIVE**

**Day 5 -- God's Menu**

Once again, we return to the importance of studying of God's Word as the primary tool for growth in all areas of our spiritual lives. Sometimes, thoughts of Bible study make us think of a duty and responsibility. Instead, think of going into our favorite restaurant and the waiter handing us a menu of choice foods and dishes. Our reaction is not one of responsibility and duty, but pure delight. When we come to the Bible, we are coming out of the world of our own cooking and going to the divine and celestial restaurant in which the menu is Truth in various servings from God Himself and the Holy Spirit. Instead of drudgery and boredom, it ought to be sheer and absolute pleasure!

The choice is between total enjoyment of eating from God's table with its incredible menu or going to the Bible as a chore to get a few more crumbs of commands to survive another hour and another day.

*"Now the Bereans were of more noble character than the Thessalonians, for they received the message with great eagerness and examined the Scriptures every day to see if what Paul said was true" (Acts 17:11).*

As you study the Bible, have an attitude of openness by which you humbly ask the Holy Spirit to reveal the truth. With a searching heart, ask questions rather than coming with preconceived notions to support your previous religious ideas. Look at every word in the entire message by observing the whole and the parts, and then put the pieces together so that you may see the entire message in a new perspective. By studying the parts, you will be able to get an increasingly clearer picture of the whole.

Jesus' attitude toward Scripture is revealed in His words, "This is what I told you while I was still with you: Everything must be fulfilled that is written about me in the Law of Moses, the Prophets and the Psalms" (Luke 24:44).

There are times when you should record who the characters are, what happened, and where it happened. Is it significant? When is the time of the event and why is it important to know? How can this passage be used today?

Many times a verse lends itself to such questions as:

- What does this tell me about God, and how should I think about Him or act toward Him?
- What does this tell me about myself, and how does this affect me and how should I act?
- What does this tell me about other people and how should I treat them?
- What does this mean to me?
- What sins are addressed?
- What blessings are promised?
- What actions should I take?

Think about how God's Word is at work in your life by making Himself known to you, by giving you life, by helping you grow, and by showing you His will, mercy and love. It contains all that we need to know spiritually, and we need no further revelation. It's a full menu which offers everything we will ever need to know about God and ourselves.

Read what the Psalmist says about God's word: *"The law of the Lord is perfect, reviving the soul. The statutes of the Lord are trustworthy, making wise the simple. The precepts of the Lord are right, giving joy to the heart. The commands of the Lord are radiant, giving light to the eyes. The fear of the Lord is pure, enduring forever. The ordinances of the LORD are sure and altogether righteous (Ps. 19:7-9)*

Many people find it helpful to keep a journal of what God is teaching them through their reading and studying of the Word. You have been journaling a little each day after your closing prayer. We will talk more about this later when we discuss prayer and meditation. One simple way to start is to pick a passage to read and ask yourself the questions above. Write what you think God is saying to you. Pray for help to address the issues He raises. You will be amazed when you return to your journal entry as God brings His power to bear in your life. Keeping a written record helps us celebrate our victories and growth in Christ.

An important aspect of Bible study is your relationship with other believers. In your small group, you will be challenged to apply the Word in your life. You need the support, encouragement and accountability of other Christians to continue your growth. Don't short-change this important aspect of your study of the Word. The ministry of others to you is important. You will also have the privilege of ministering the Word to others.

*"Let us not give up meeting together, as some are in the habit of doing, but let us encourage one another -- and all the more as you see the Day approaching" (Heb. 10:25).*

**What problems can you expect to encounter in your plan for a regular Bible study and for belonging to a study group?**

Give thanks that God loves you so much and wants you to know His will for your life. After your time of prayer, spend a minute in silence. Record any thoughts you might have below.

**WEEK FIVE**

**Major Points to Review**

1.  Why should we be baptized and when should baptism occur?

2.  Baptism offers great power and encouragement for daily living.  What is the source of this power?

3.  What do you believe regarding Christ's presence during communion?

4.  What is the basis of your worship of God?

**OBSERVATIONS/REFLECTIONS ON WHAT YOU STUDIED THIS WEEK:**

1.  What matters or issues would you like to know more about?  What, if anything, troubled you about what you studied?

2.  What new knowledge or insights have you learned?

**WEEK FIVE**                                    

3.      How has your faith grown or been modified?


4.      How will this affect your life?

# WEEK SIX

# MY LIFE AS JESUS' SERVANT

The question of what we do with our lives is answered from being sons and daughters of God, growing to spiritual maturity and showing the fruit of the Spirit in our lives. Your experience with the "Spiritual Travel Guide" will show you it is God who called you on this journey of faith to go where He leads. We must wrestle with being obedient to go where He calls us, not letting our sinful self limit God's plan for our lives.

*What do you think is God's purpose for your life?*

*How can you become the person God intends you to be?*

## Day One -- My Christian Calling

Believers are "God's representatives", and as such God has a plan for each of them. As He once selected Abraham and told him, "I will bless you...and you will be a blessing"(Genesis 12:2), so He has given us His love and mercy to serve others in His name. We are His "sent ones" or "called ones" who experienced a miraculous change in our existence when God came into our lives.

The call is an act of God's grace in which Jesus takes the initiative, *"You did not choose Me, but I chose you and appointed you to go and bear fruit that will last" (John 15:16).*

We are valued, loved, called and appointed by the God of heaven and earth.  We are God's people regardless of our gifts, performance or rank.  Colossians 1:1-18 informs us of who we are by God's grace, to whom we belong, what has been done for us, to what we have been called, and the unlimited power available to us.  This Gospel has much to say about the complex issues of good and evil facing us.  We have been liberated from a self-justifying religion by God's call of grace.  The Word and baptism are the communicators of this new life in Christ.

*How does the Gospel give hope for being faithful to our calling?*

Paul is concerned that Christians understand the blessing of God's call, *"I pray also that the eyes of your heart may be enlightened in order that you may know the hope to which He has called you, the riches of His glorious inheritance in the saints, and His incomparably great power for us who believe..." (Eph. 1:18-19).*

Then Paul adds, "I urge you to live a life worthy of the calling you have received"(Eph. 4:1).  This call is based upon Christ's righteousness given to us who believe.  This call is not only to be right with God, but also to live righteously in the will of God.

*What does Eph. 4:1 mean for the decisions you make?  How should your calling in Christ affect your life this week?*

**WEEK SIX**

We are powerless to obey this call without the work of the Holy Spirit. It is dangerous to ignore the Holy Spirit or quench Him (1 Thes. 5:19). Dependence upon the Spirit will assure our positive response to the call.

*In what ways can or do you say "no" to your Christian calling?*

God's call does not take us out of the world, but leaves us in it with definite functions in the world and in the church. Our business is to represent God and to share His love in our relationship with everyone.

*What does it mean to live in the world but not be of the world?*

The Christian calling puts everything into focus: the place of the Word, how we relate to Christ our Savior and Lord, and how we choose our lifestyle and our commitment to service. Christ's call will provide the right answers to the many questions we may have about fulfilling our purpose in life.

1. *What assurance can we gain from Psalm 139:16 that God truly has a plan for us individually?*

2. *How does the Gospel give us hope to be faithful to our calling?*

**WEEK SIX**

Go to God in prayer and ask him to guide you and knowing and performing your call from him do travel this world as a Christian in a foreign land. After your time of prayer, spend a minute in silence. Record any thoughts you might have below.

## Day Two -- We Are Made In God's Image

Genesis 1:27, 5:1 and James 3:9 tell us that human beings are made in the image or likeness of God. God's original intent was that we as His creatures be like Him, and that is still His goal for us. Being created in the image of God means that we are spiritual beings related to our Father/Creator with reflections of His nature. We are moral beings who by the Holy Spirit's help can know right from wrong and can make moral choices. The question is whether He is our Maker, and whether we are controlled and empowered by Him or not.

The meaning of being sons and daughters of God was clear to the Old Testament believers, but its depth of meaning is not easy to understand for us unless we know what it meant to be a son, especially a firstborn. If we do not recognize this, we will miss much of what God intended in our relationship with Him. Sonship constituted a person's very identity that shaped his entire life. God wants us to enjoy Him in a way that typifies the proper relationship between a father and son (or daughter), a family resemblance, including women as daughters of God. Our sonship received from Adam was flawed, but Jesus was the way God used to restore us to His original purpose as sons and daughters. The first Adam gave us sin, and the second Adam (Jesus) gave us life.

We must recognize the difference between what we inherited through Adam and through God in Jesus. As God created the human race through one man, He recreated them through the second Man (Jesus), who came to restore what God had wanted to do for all time through our human father Adam (Galatians 3:26).  We experience God's original purpose for us in and through Jesus Christ, which also includes the adoption of His daughters.

The Fall into sin changed our image, but through regeneration some of this is restored as we are related to our holy and loving God.  The fallen person is still partly an image-bearer of God.

*What does it mean to you to be created in God's image? What limits did the Fall of man put on us growing as God's children in His image?*

*How have you felt these limits in your own life?*

The thought that Christians need continually to grow toward being conformed in the image of God is seen in the Scriptures that speak of putting off the old man and putting on the new man, which is being renewed in the image of the Creator (Col. 3:9-10).  Even though our image has been distorted by the Fall, we Christians still possess the gifts and capacities with which God has endowed us, though also used in sinful and disobedient ways.

The perversion of this image has affected our functioning in three relationships into which God has placed us: worship (now tempted to worship idols); fellowship (now often using gifts to manipulate others as tools for selfish purposes); the relationship between us and nature (instead of mastering the world for God, we now attempt to use the world and its resources for our selfish purposes).

The entire Christian life has to be understood in terms of growing in the likeness of God, having been adopted through the new birth as His sons and daughters. The adoption as God's children is seen in the first words of the Lord's Prayer (Matthew 6:9), "Our Father...". This leads to imitating the Father: "...That you may be sons of your Father in heaven...Be perfect, therefore, as your heavenly Father is perfect"(Matthew 5:45-48). This does not mean we can be perfect in our actions, but that our deeds should glorify and please the Father (Matthew 5:16; 6:1).

*What is involved in being conformed to the image of God? How do you show this in your life?*


The renewed image by our new birth enables us to direct ourselves toward God and be empowered to love our neighbor and be good managers of nature. This means that we are to mirror God and to represent Him, doing what He desires. This renewal of the image is never completed in our lifetime, but is a process that continues as long as we live (sanctification).

Human beings left to themselves repudiate the true God and go into the "god" business by trying to run their own lives their own way. They choose what they want and decide for themselves what is right and wrong.

Our lives united with the life of God through faith in Christ must be strongly related to our eternal destiny as our hope for the future. Being in the image of God directs our mind to focus on our purpose and what we offer the world.

**WEEK SIX**                                    **117**

Our true selves and image is Christ in us. That's what others should see in us as Christians. Our self image should never be derived from our old nature, our actions and performance - what we do. Rather, our self-esteem should come from the reality that we are new creatures in whom Christ lives through daily forgiveness. Our only pride should be the cross of Christ.

***On what should Christians base their self-image if they are to glorify God?***

Go to God in prayer and ask Him to make you fully aware of His image in you through baptism, and to help you set proper goals for refinding Christ in your life. After you time of prayer, spend a minute in silence. Record any thoughts you might have below.

## Day Three -- The Fierce Struggle Between Our Old and New Natures

If we are to win the battles of life, we must know the nature of its conflict or struggle. The fight is between our old and our new selves, sometimes called the old and new nature, old and new man, or sinner and saint.

We were born into the world with only one nature - the sinful one as the old self. Romans 7:18 reminds us that in that nature there is nothing good in us - we are totally corrupt. We must recognize that this old nature is a complete spiritual being.

We are not half old nature and half new nature. Our old self is one hundred percent, totally, a spiritual being with it's own identity.

*How did we get the old nature, old self, or old man?*


What happened that the Christian also has a new nature or is a new self? This occurs in our baptism or new birth, as Christ comes into our lives as a new nature, a new identity, a new spiritual being. This spiritual being is holy and perfect, created by the miracle of baptism in us.

1. *How did we get the new nature, new man?*



2. *What are we do to according to Eph. 4:22-24; what are we to put off and what are we to put on?*



We have two natures: our bodies are the home of two completely opposite spiritual beings - one who wants to destroy us and the other to help us enjoy God now and for eternity.

The devil's contact with the believer is through the old nature or Old Adam only. Satan has no access to the new nature received in baptism and redemption. Any control over the Christian is by permission or by individual surrender to the devil. Christians are free to choose which of the two natures will control them.

**WEEK SIX**                                        

1. *What choices have you made this week under the influence of the old self?*

2. *How have these choices affected your life?*

The center of spiritual warfare which Satan utilizes through the old self is our mind, where the thought-life is laid open to his inspection. He seeks to take away or dilute the Word in order to introduce his own ideas. He has the definite advantage of instant and immediate access to each person's mind to see the complete panorama of our thoughts and imaginations, being familiar with any weakness and strength. He knows our vulnerable areas and our secret ambitions and longings.

*How have you grown in your ability to discern Satan's lies? Do you need help in this area of your Christian life?*

Believers are the battleground between two masters, both seeking control. We are really two beings at the same time - the old self and the new self, sinner and saint. Unbelievers are sinners only, but Christians are simultaneously sinner-saints, old nature-new nature. Both are complete spiritual beings, fighting against each other. That's why Paul could say that he was entirely sinful and entirely holy before God, sinner and saint at the same time. *"For the sinful nature desires what is contrary to the Spirit, and the Spirit what is contrary to the sinful nature. They*

**WEEK SIX**                                    **120**

*are in conflict with each other, so that you do not do what you want" (Gal. 5:17).*

*How intense do we expect this fight to be? Are signs of a battle good or bad? Why?*


As we feed on the Word and communicate with God in prayer, we will experience the enabling power of the Holy Spirit to strengthen and sanctify us through and through (1 Thes. 5:23). The fruit of the Word and prayers for holiness help put to death whatever belongs to our earthly nature (Col. 3:5). The issue is not that we will not sin anymore, but that we will not be slaves or controlled by sinful habits (Rom. 6:6).

*What does Paul say about the conflict between the old man and new man in his life in Rom. 7:15-25? How does Paul's courageous and victorious struggle encourage you?*


Go to God in prayer and ask Him to give you strength for the spiritual war waging inside you between the old and new natures. After your time of prayer, spend a minute in silence. Record any thoughts you might have below.


## Day Four -- Our Old Nature of Sin

The old nature (old man or old self) reveals itself in a lifestyle that is enslaved to sin. It is disobedient, arrogant, undisciplined, ignorant, doubts God and God's Word, lusts after worldly assets, and is a slave to the devil. At times the old self shows itself by excesses and enslaving habits, even immorality. Another characteristic is self-justification, finding it difficult to admit making mistakes, being slow to apologize and often rationalizing.

There's also self-sufficiency in which we depend upon our own wisdom, ability and effort instead of relying entirely on the resources and grace of God. Another damaging trait is self-will, where we go our own way instead of seeking God's will in every decision and area of life.

*Search the following Bible passages and find details about the old nature, its character, actions and what we should do about it:*

| | |
|---|---|
| Eph. 4:22 | |
| Gal. 5:16 | |
| Gal. 5:19-21 | |
| Gal. 3:2, 5-8 | |
| Rom. 6:11 | |
| Rom. 6:12-13 | |
| Rom. 8:6 | |

1.   *What are some of the evil things which the old self does, which you see in our community today? Are any observed in Christians of our area?*

**WEEK SIX**                                   122

2. *Who instructs the old self?  Who makes the decisions to control the old  self?*


Go to God in prayer and ask Him to help you understand how your old nature is fighting against every good thing that you desire.  After your time of prayer, spend a minute in silence. Record any thoughts you might have below.


## Day Five -- Victory Through My New Nature in Christ

The new nature or new self came into being through our baptism and reveals itself in a new lifestyle that is joyfully obedient to God.  The Christ-identity in us is aware of the truth, alive to Christ, dead to the world, obedient, pious, and disciplined. Paul calls on Christians to make their lives consistent with the new selves they have put on in baptism: "...Do you not realize that Christ Jesus is in you?..."(2 Cor. 13:5).

The new nature focuses on love from God and to others. The new nature recognizes God's gifts and the Holy Spirit.

*Please write what you find in the following Scriptures about the character and activities of the new nature or new self, and what we are to do:*

| Ephesians 4:24 | |
| --- | --- |
| Eph. 4:32 | |
| Gal. 5:16 | |

| Gal. 5:22-25 | |
| --- | --- |
| Col. 3:2, 12-13 | |

Who will be in control and who will be master?  It all depends on which we feed - the old or the new self.  If we deceive ourselves and rationalize our lifestyle, we will feed on spiritual garbage and poison which gushes forth from our culture, its publications and media.  The old nature needs to be starved, not fed.

At the same time, we must feed the new nature by regular Bible study, by reading and studying in our homes, and in our small groups.  Our private and public worship will be the food that strengthens our new nature for the battles of life.  Fellow Christians will aid us.

*How do the old self and new self present two different world views? How do they contrast?*

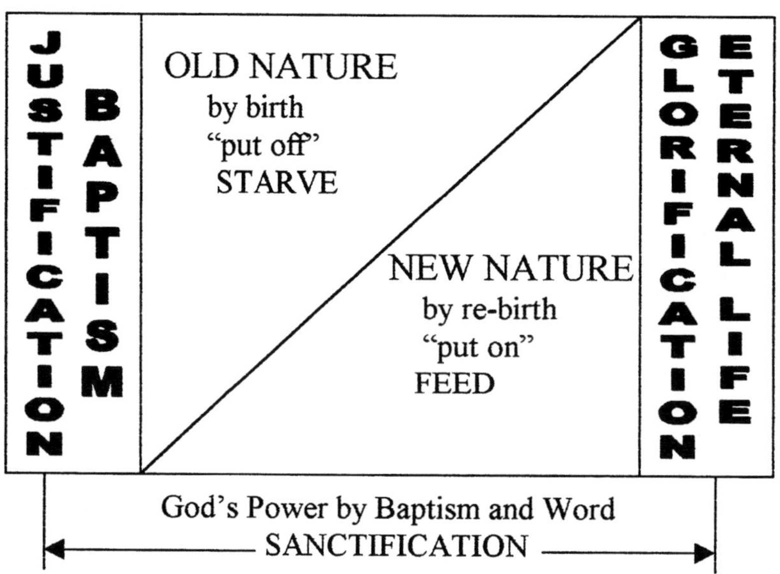


There are no ten easy lessons to gain victory over the old nature or how sinful habits can be changed into godly discipline. The solution lies in starving the old self, then a solid feeding program of the new self through the Gospel. Feeding the new nature involves believing what God has said about learning how this enemy operates, adopting a definite plan of resisting him, and knowing how to use our resources in Christ.

1. *What are ways in which we can feed the old self?*


2. *In what ways can we starve the new self?*


**WEEK SIX**                                          

*3. Why is it vital that every Christian should have a clear knowledge and understanding of the activity of the old nature and the new nature working inside?*

Most Christians today do not have a strong plan to feed the new nature. Their spiritual growth and health is left to chance, making them very susceptible to Satan's attacks. We all need a regular diet of the Word to keep strong for our battles. How we approach our intake of the Word is critical.
*What is your view of everyday feeding compared to once-a-week feeding on the Word?*

Our lives must be open to God's Word through a variety of inputs. Other Christians are important sources of encouragement and teaching. Close relationships with other Christians allow us to be honest about ourselves in ways we would not attempt in larger group settings. We allow the Word to touch those parts of our lives that we protect in public. Open yourself to the ministry of the Word through those close to you that have traveled a step or two ahead you. You will find great encouragement from their experience.

Go to God in prayer and ask Him to give you new victories for your new nature over your old nature. After your time of prayer, spend a minute in silence. Record any thoughts you might have below.

**Major Points to Review**

1.  *How would you describe God's call to you today?*


2.  *We are made in God's image. The Fall has changed our image. Through God's grace some of God's image is restored in our lives. How have you felt God restoring His image in you?*


3.  *We must contend with a fierce battle between our old and new natures. Satan only has access to our old nature. At the same time God is working in our new nature. How do you sense the struggle between these two natures in your life?*


4.  *Why and how should we identify and avoid being enslaved to sinful habits?*


5.  *Our victory is through our new nature in Christ. What is your plan to feed your new nature and starve your old nature?*

## OBSERVATIONS/REFLECTIONS ON WHAT YOU STUDIED THIS WEEK:

1. What matters or issues would you like to know more about? What, if anything, troubled you about what you studied?

2. What new knowledge or insights have you learned?

3. How has your faith grown or been modified?

4. How will this affect your life?

# WEEK SEVEN

# KEEPING RIGHT WITH GOD AND BEING FULLY ASSURED OF SALVATION

This week we are facing the big issue of life – our certainty of being saved!  All else depends on that!

## Day One -- No Performance-Based Acceptance by God

When we become Christians, a spiritual battle begins with great intensity.  The devil wants our relationship with Christ to be lukewarm.  His favorite strategy is to raise doubts about the certainty of salvation.  Research has shown for many years that over half of all Christians are not certain of being saved!  They believe they must win God's approval by proper behavior and by doing good deeds.  They do not fully realize their salvation has been completely won by the full sacrifice of Jesus Christ on the Cross.  There is nothing they can do to make it more certain. Christ has done it all.

Think of it: over half of all Christians seem to think that their redemption is conditional -- conditioned by what they can do through church membership and activities.  This is an issue that we must settle!  The result of perceiving that God's love is conditional is "Performance-Based Acceptance (PBA)."

If we buy the PBA lie of Satan, we seek our worth in what we do.  Our identity becomes tied to our actions.  We never realize the promise of self-based worth because we can never do enough.  Our life is reduced to a struggle to produce results for God.  Instead of recognizing God's love for us -- His creation, we seek to establish our value by what we do for God.  Such activism makes busyness, not God, the goal of a Christian life.

PBA is an attempt to seek our worth and acceptance by God through what we do.  The problem is that we never know how many deeds are enough to please God.  Life then is reduced to actions and results, the only way we can appease God and measure our value.  Such activism makes spiritual busyness, not God, the goal of religious life.

Performance-Based Acceptance (PBA) is an ugly intrusion into the free grace of God and the unconditional love of Christ and the forgiveness of all our sins.  It is a terrible perversion of the free gift of the precious Gospel of Jesus Christ.  If we do not recognize and stop it, its many tentacles will begin to develop in our lives until our whole life is based on Performance-Based Acceptance.

1.   *Write your own definition of PBA here:*

2.   *Why do we tend to depend more on ourselves by doing good deeds for our salvation than on God's grace and the Holy Spirit's power?*

PBA is a form of "salvation by works."  It programs us to be manipulators as we are in bondage to those that we seek to impress for acceptance.  This creates depression and anxiety that is  humanly  unbearable.     It  hurts  us  emotionally  and psychologically. It cripples us with fear, stress and pressure. The gift of grace seems too good to be true. We tend to try to do something to show our appreciation, which we believe God will then credit to our account. But Performance-Based Christians do not really feel good about themselves, in spite of what they have accomplished. They are always worrying about maintaining their performance.

1. *Tell about a time you were motivated to do something because you felt it was required behavior as a "good" Christian. How do you feel about this action today?*


2. *The insidious nature of PBA is that it never answers many questions. Have you found yourself asking any of the following questions (check any that apply)?*

— *How much performance is necessary from me to be accepted by God?*

— *Who sets my standard for performance, and how will the performance be measured?*

— *Will the expectations for my performance always be changing or will they be set and rigid?*

— *How will I know when I have achieved full acceptance by God?*

— *What will I have to do tomorrow or the next day to achieve and keep God's acceptance?*

— *How long will what I have worked to achieve today last?*

God did not say, "I love you since you go to church and try to do good." He did not say, "I will love you if or when you meet My expectations." Any such statement makes God's love conditional, which means that it was caused by something in us -- our goodness or our attractiveness. God's love is unconditional. It flows out of Him because of His holy nature. Why should we carry this heavy load of doubt when the Holy Spirit, the ultimate Spiritual Counselor/Therapist, desires to solve our personal problems?

*"Why are you downcast, oh my soul? Why so distressed within me? Put your hope in God, for I will yet praise Him, my Savior and my God" (Psalm 42:11). "Come to Me, all you who are weary and burdened, and I will give you rest" (Matt. 11:28).*

**What is damaging about PBA and behavioral Christianity?**




Go to God in prayer and ask him to help you deal with any temptations toward PBA in your life. After your time of prayer, spend a minute in silence. Record any thoughts you might have below.




**Day Two -- Everything is Resolved in Repentance--Forgiveness**

Instead of suffering with a PBA problem, we need to grow in our understanding of God's plan for repentance, forgiveness and reconciliation. The more we understand this wonderful gift, the less we are trapped by Satan in PBA. The result is freedom. What we do is motivated by who we are -- a forgiven child of God. We come to grips with the fact that our

**WEEK SEVEN**                                          **132**

best is not good enough for God.  We don't have to drag our failures around with us as we go through life.  What has been broken or destroyed by our wrong actions is repaired by God's loving process of repentance, forgiveness and reconciliation.  This means that we stop excusing ourselves or claiming that our intentions were good.  Instead, we learn to rest in God's grace given to us through Christ.  We come to rely on His performance instead of our own.

This does not allow us to turn a blind eye toward our sin. Instead, we let God's grace deal with sin in our lives while living with complete assurance of God's acceptance of us.  The more we understand God's grace, the more willing we are to let God deal with sin in our lives.  The first step in this process is repentance.

*We can best understand repentance when we have a firm grasp of the concept of sin.  What do the following verses say about sin?*

| | |
|---|---|
| Gen. 8:21 | |
| Ps. 51:5 | |
| Rom.7:18-24 | |
| 1 John 3:4 | |
| Gal. 5:19-21 | |
| James 4:17 | |
| Rom. 6:23 | |

**WEEK SEVEN**                                   133

*With this understanding of sin, how would you define the word repentance?*

No matter how many wrong turns we may have taken in life, God always welcomes us back.  God welcomes U-turns at any time on our human road of life when we have sinned.  Sometimes he requires a right turn or a left turn, but it is always a turn away from sin.  Often God gives us a yield sign, either yielding to another person but especially to God when we need to say, "Not my will, but Yours be done!" As Jesus did, we should always yield to the will of God.

Sometimes we get off on a road that is a dead-end, or another road with dangerous curves.  Sometimes we are not careful at dangerous intersections or we are not alert at the many distractions as we travel the road of life.  When we exceed God's specific speed limit, the law indicates the traffic tickets, but the Gospel shows us that Jesus pays them all.  Some drivers think that they can avoid traffic tickets by using radar detectors.  They want to break the speed limit and then slow down before getting caught.  Some get away with this, but they cannot sin against God and still avoid His detection.  They way to unmask evil is to face reality by recognizing our wrong and repenting.

Repentance allows us to renounce what is bad.  It requires a change of mind, heart and conduct.  Sorrow over sins is not enough, for there needs to be a change in the inward condition of our minds and hearts.  People can be sorry for being caught and being deprived of the pleasures of sin, but that is not repentance.

See the difference between worldly and godly sorrow shown in the chart below:

| Worldly Sorrow | Godly Sorrow |
| --- | --- |
| Encourages us to try to pay for sin | Causes us to confess our inability to repay God for His blessings and to joyfully declare that Jesus has already done it |
| Causes us to recognize that punishment is required, so we may even try to punish ourselves | Recognizes that Jesus has already taken our punishment -- that there is no more punishment needed |
| Tries to gain right-standing through meeting man's expectation for punishment | Recognizes that we cannot justify ourselves, for God has already made us right with Himself |
| Self-centered | God-centered |

God wants us to repent. Read the following verses. What do they say about our need to repent?

| Jer. 5:3-4 | |
| --- | --- |
| Mark 1:15 | |
| Luke 13:3 | |
| Acts 3:19 | |
| Acts 17:30 | |

*Is God overdoing it by His insistent demands for daily repentance? Why or why not?*

**WEEK SEVEN**                    **135**

Genuine repentance does not involve the mere giving up of sins, but includes growing in freedom from slavery to sin. This means that we allow the Holy Spirit to work through sin issues in our lives. We seek to be set free from the bondage of sin. It is a process that continues throughout our lives and is never complete until we reach Heaven. We call this process sanctification. Sanctification means God is setting us apart, making us holy for His purposes. As we grow in this area God presents us with more opportunities to do His work and experience His plan for our lives.

*Why is the practice of repentance difficult in our day when cultural influences have affected our understanding of sin?*

*How does God's forgiveness of all your sins change your desire to continue in sin?*

As we grow in our understanding of God's unlimited capacity to forgive, we are moved to be more obedient to Him, to deal with sin in our life. It is not our action that earns God's forgiveness and blessings. He has made these available to us without cost. Our obedience does not make us more acceptable to Him. Our do-it-yourself world needs to learn that human efforts are utterly useless to win God's approval.

Confession of sin and faith in Christ reassures us of our forgiven condition before God. We are guilty of sin, but our guilt has been given to Christ. We stand in remorse as we grow in our understanding that Christ has removed our guilt. The Holy Spirit continues to work in us to help us see and repent of sin. Confession and faith in Christ are the keys to recovery from sinful habits and broken relationships. Through forgiveness a person enters a cleansing process that is life-renewing and energizing.

*"If we confess our sins, He is faithful and just and will forgive us our sins and purify us from all unrighteousness" (1 John. 1:9).* Confession and faith in Jesus help us to dispose of our spiritual garbage.

Confessing our sins and receiving the gift of forgiveness is a promise of the Father, a provision of the Son, a proclamation of the Holy Spirit in the Word and a practice of a Christian. God's love and forgiveness pays our debts and restores us to a healthy relationship with Him.

*Sometimes we fail to admit that we suffer from certain types of sin. We may excuse ourselves from repenting for a variety of reasons (i.e., "I'm not as bad as . . .). How may you have excused yourself from repentance of a sin?*

*Sometimes we fail to see our sins. Spend a minute now and ask God to guide you to areas where He would like to eliminate sin. Read Ps. 139:23-24.*

We have been restored to a whole new life. Let us enjoy having been made right with God. Rejoice that our debt has been canceled! Shout that God's love has triumphed over His law! Let's enjoy forgiveness!

**WEEK SEVEN**                                           **137**

*Are you ever tempted to think that God does not or will not fully and completely forgive every sin?  How does this affect your relationship with God?*

Go to God in prayer and ask Him to help you recognize at all times the great gift He has given you in daily repentance and forgiveness in Christ.  After your time of prayer, spend a minute in silence.  Record any thoughts you might have below.

## Day Three -- My Self-Worth In Christ

To feel bad about ourselves and maintain the lowest possible opinion is not true Christian humility.  That can be a spiritual problem that does not take into consideration God's restoration of our image of Him through Jesus' indwelling. Low self-esteem can be an emotional problem that creates an inability to receive praise and encouragement because we may feel that we are not worthy of it.  A strong negative ego can cause us to be so self-centered that we will be individualistic, devoid of any interest in others.

Another condition from which we suffer is being overly concerned about what others believe and feel about us. Sometimes we then want to conform and be who others want us to be.  This means that when we are praised by others, we feel great, and when we are not, we feel small.  Then we think we must conform to others' expectations of what is valuable in order to feel valuable.  This kind of conformism distorts our relationships and weakens or garbles our sense of identity so that we become

**WEEK SEVEN**                    138

dependent on other individuals or the group for our sense of worth.

Naturally, we have a drive to be recognized, but when it takes the twisted form of being conformed, we become insecure, needing to take a poll to see how others are rating us today. This causes us to be chameleons, for how we see ourselves depends on the group of people we happen to be with. We adopt values and tastes from those around us. As we bend and shape our convictions and conduct in order to fit in, it is hard to have deep relationships, and it weakens our ability to stand against the pressures of the world.

1.  *What do you learn from Exodus 4:10-17 about Moses' self-image? How does Moses' view of himself differ from God's perspective? In what way can a poor self-image become sin?*

2.  *Read Genesis 5:1 and James 3:9. How does our self-image depend upon our understanding of God and our faith in Him?*

It is also possible for our old self to produce a spirit of pride and superiority, being puffed up, inflated and haughty, which are destructive substitutes for genuine self-acceptance.

*What do the following verses in 1 Corinthians say about our potential for sinful self-centeredness?*

| | |
|---|---|
| *4:5* | |
| *4:18-19* | |
| *5:2* | |
| *8:1* | |
| *13:4* | |

Sinful self-centeredness focuses on appearances, position, status, ability and financial resources.

How then are we to think of ourselves? Clearly, we are to avoid the extremes of relying on others opinions of us to determine our self worth and sinful self-centeredness. The answer is found in who we are in Christ. With the trademark of the Master Designer upon us, we are a divine original -- something special and unique. We are distinct from others and must not try to be somebody else. We must dare to be ourselves. God never intended us to be another person, for trying to do that makes us phonies. We should never be caught in the comparison games, but accept ourselves for who we are in Christ. If God so loved us, how dare we not love what God loves: ourselves as unique individuals? High self-worth identified in Christ is totally consistent with the humble spirit that Jesus asked His followers to display.

We are more than flesh and bones. We are the product of God's creation and re-creation in Christ. This gives us our spiritual perspective on life and our worth. We should see ourselves as God sees us through His miracle of regeneration, and accept ourselves as God accepts us in Christ. A sound root system in Christ creates good character and productivity. Not loving ourselves comes from believing wrongly about ourselves. We should not operate on the basis of other people's distortions or under a false understanding of forgiveness.

Even with a deep sense of sin, Paul was able to maintain a predominantly positive self-image, which was in God, not in himself. His positive statements about himself reflected his expression of his new nature:

*"By the grace of God, I am what I am, and His grace to me was not without effect. No, I worked harder than all of them -- not I, but the grace of God that was with me" (1 Cor. 15:10). "Such confidence as this is ours through Christ, before God. Not that we are competent in ourselves to claim anything for ourselves, but our competence comes from God" (2 Cor. 3:4-5).*

God makes us qualified and gives us great worth. With Paul, we can boast of nothing but Jesus Christ (1 Cor. 1:30-31). Paul was realistic about his strength and weaknesses because he had a healthy self-image. God's grace not only built Paul's character, but also influenced positive change in his personality and temperament.

*What is wrong with having false humility or putting ourselves down instead of rating ourselves on the basis of Christ-in-us?*

Jesus Christ is the greatest value and worth in the world. He lives in all Christians, and he gives us the greatest worth. That gives us high self-esteem. The more we grow in His plan for our lives, the more we will experience an understanding of self. Our self-image will grow as we participate in God's work and watch

Him work through us to affect the lives of others.  With God always ready to forgive us when we fall short of His expectations, we are free to serve Him without fear.  We know that no matter how well or poor we perform, God's love and forgiveness never change.

Go to God in prayer and ask Him to give you constant/consistent  high horse or high self-esteem in Christ. After your time of prayer, spend a minute in silence.  Record any thoughts you might have below.


## Day Four – Being Certain of Being Saved

The love of God and His ability to accept us are based on grace, not on our ability to impress Him with deeds.  Christ offers us unconditional love and healing, even of our emotions.  We do not have to please God in exchange for His acceptance of us. Even in failure, the repentant Christian is deeply loved by God, completely forgiven, totally accepted by God and complete in Christ.

*Think about a time when you may have doubted your salvation.  Considering what you have learned this week, which lie was Satan using in his attack on your peace as a Christian?*


Even with the assurances we have from the Word, doubt creeps in and tries to steal the peace that God intends for us. Sometimes we are burdened with the guilt of our sins. We feel that our sins in the past were so bad that we doubt God could ever forgive them. How could God really love such a sinner? Consider Romans 5:8-11:

*"But God demonstrates his own love for us in this: While we were yet sinners, Christ died for us. Since we have now been justified by His blood, how much more shall we be saved from God's wrath through Him! For if when we were God's enemies we were reconciled to Him through the death of His Son, how much more, having been reconciled, shall we be saved through His life! Not only is this so, but we also rejoice in God through our Lord Jesus Christ, to whom we have now received reconciliation."*

God's action to save us was taken when we were still His enemies. God didn't wait for us to clean up our act to send His Son. Jesus' death was a payment in advance for all sin no matter how bad the sin seems to us. Our full and complete salvation is the foundation of our living hope that our salvation is assured.

***Our repentance means stopping our sinful habits and to change. Why would failure to stop or to change cause us to feel half-guilty, despite God's Word of forgiveness?***

The farther we are from Him, the more difficult it is to hear His plan of forgiveness through Christ. As we grow in our understanding of God's capacity for forgiveness, we grow in our understanding of the security of our salvation. It is this gift of faith that saves us.

"In His great mercy, He has given us new birth into a living hope through the resurrection of Jesus Christ from the dead"(1 Peter 1:3). When Jesus ascended into heaven, he assured us that He is our redeemer and that we will live forever with Him:

"In My Father's house are many rooms; if it were not so, I would have told you.  I am going there to prepare a place for you.  And if I go and prepare a place for you, I will come back and take you to be with Me that you also may be where I am"(John 14:2-3).

What was impossible for us to do has been done by our Savior, Jesus.  Each one of us can and must be certain our sins are fully forgiven, all our guilt has been removed and that we will live with God eternally in heaven.  Our salvation is certain. Rejoice!

Go to God in prayer and thank Him that Jesus is complete payment for your salvation, and that nothing more is demanded of you, and that you are totally accepted by Him. After your time of prayer, spend a minute in silence.  Record any thoughts you might have below.

## Day Five -- The Flow of Grace

Titus 2:11-14 shows grace to have a double dimension -- grace/unmerited love for salvation and grace/power for sanctification:

*"For the grace of God that brings salvation has appeared to all men.  It teaches us to say 'no' to ungodliness and worldly passions, and to live self-controlled, upright and godly lives in this present age, while we wait for the blessed hope - the glorious appearing of our great God and Savior, Jesus Christ, Who gave Himself for us to redeem us from all wickedness and to purify for Himself a people that are His very own, eager to do what is good."*

1.  *Which of the phrases in this passage are justification?*

2.  *Which of the phrases in this passage are sanctification?*

God's grace is totally (100%) responsible for our redemption. God's grace is totally (100%) responsible for giving us the strength for doing good works. Grace flows from justification to sanctification. In fact, it is more than a flow: it is a gush of God's great grace. It is a gushing forth of God's extravagant love to save us and to empower us for living for Him. This is seen in Paul's message to Titus: *"When the kindness and love of God our Savior appeared, He saved us, not because of righteous things we had done, but because of His mercy. He saved us through the washing of rebirth and renewal of the Holy Spirit, having been justified by His grace, we might become heirs having the hope of eternal life"* (3:4-5, 7). That's justification! *"...Those who have trusted in God be careful to devote themselves to doing what is good..."* (Titus 3:8). That's sanctification!

1.  *What part does God have and what part do we have in our justification?*

2.  *What part does God have and what part do we have in our sanctification?*

Eph. 2:8-10 says that "For it is by grace you have been saved, through faith--and this not from yourselves, it is the gift of God-

**WEEK SEVEN**                                                    **145**

not of works, so that no one can boast," and continues: "For we are God's workmanship, created in Christ Jesus to do good works, which God prepared in advance for us to do."  Once again, Paul presents two functions of grace which flow from God's unmerited love and His power.

The dynamic nature of grace for living the Christian life is offered in 2 Cor. 9:8, "God is able to make all grace abound to you, so that in all things at all times, having all that you need, you will abound in every good work."

Grace is:

- Strength for our weaknesses so that we can serve God.
- Our only hope for dealing with any problem or sinful habit.
- The only power that can destroy and conquer the destructiveness of any bondage.
- The force for freedom.  Any unresolved slavery is an enemy of grace.
- The bridge to transformation and reformation to get away from the land of slavery where we try repeatedly to make ourselves holy on our own terms.

Nothing in our culture prepares us for the radical reality of grace or God's kindness.  We live in a culture where the prevailing thought pattern is that people are rewarded solely on performance.  Grace says that we get what we don't deserve -- forgiveness instead of punishment for sins.  This goes completely against the grain of our society today.

The facts of grace are simple, even in their double dimension. Grace is a pure gift which always exists.  It is always available and good, coming often at surprising times to catch us off-guard when our manipulative systems are working furiously to achieve our own desires and goals in our own way.  This amazing grace simply will not allow us to be in control, for it is God's love in action.  Grace is the dynamic outpouring of God's loving nature that flows in and through the believer in an endless flow of mercy, healing and power.

We cannot accept grace if our hands are full of earthly things to which we are enslaved.  If our minds and hearts are filled with cultural influences, they are polluted and permeated with things that shut out grace, occupying and congesting spaces where grace should flow.  Hearts, minds and hands can be emptied of these destructive things only through repentance and forgiveness.

The Bible warns us that we can misuse this gift of grace:*"As God's fellow workers, we urge you not to receive God's grace in vain "*( 2 Cor. 6:1).

One of the joys of grace is that we have the opportunity to share grace with other people.   1 Peter 4:10 tells, *"Each one should use whatever gift he has received to serve others, faithfully, administering God's grace in its various forms."*

There is no other experience on this planet more awesome than being used to do God's work!  Many Christians today live out a lukewarm relationship with their Savior, and are afraid to move forward in ministry because they are afraid of what God might ask of them.  They forget, however, the power of God's grace to create change within them.  God promises to give us the strength to live in this way of service and ministry.

1. *In what ways does Phil. 4:13 show the pursuit of holiness to be a venture between God and Christians?*

2. *Study 1 Cor. 3:10 and 15:10 and 2 Cor. 9:8.  Why do some Christians fully accept grace as causing salvation, but find it difficult to accept God's full grace in the area of sanctification or living the Christian life?*

**Major Points to Review**

1. *As God's children we must escape Satan's PBA lie and understand God's complete, unconditional acceptance of us. How may you experience PBA?*

2. *The cycle of repentance, forgiveness and reconciliation should be experienced daily by us. How do you get in the way of this process? What variants can prevent us from enjoying this cycle or process?*

3. *Self-esteem, false humility, conformism and self-centeredness have a negative effect on our proper self-image in Christ. As you observe Christians and yourself, which of these sins are we struggling most with in our day?*

4. *Research has shown that half of all Christians today are uncertain of their salvation. What should we in our church do about this?*

5. *According to Titus 2:11-14, grace impacts our spiritual lives in two dimensions - justification and sanctification. What happens when some Christians see grace only for salvation, but forget about or ignore sanctification?*

**OBSERVATIONS/REFLECTIONS ON WHAT YOU STUDIED THIS WEEK:**

1. What matters or issues would you like to know more about? What, if anything, troubled you about what you studied?

2. What new knowledge or insights have you learned?

3. How has your faith grown or been modified?

4. How will this affect your life?

# WEEK EIGHT

# SPIRITUAL WARFARE

It is not surprising that there is a lot of talk today about spiritual warfare. Fierce spiritual warfare has been unleashed in the world today and has left some Christians confused. As you grow in your relationship with God, you will want to understand all that you can about resisting Satan and his band of demons. You don't want to enter into this battle without the proper equipment or training.

In our battles of life, we need more than work clothes or traveling clothes. Sometimes we need war clothes for protection against the devil's evil ways. Soft cloth fabric is not enough, but strong armor is required. Let's consider how we can be prepared for this war.

## Day One -- The Spiritual Battle of Life

Have you ever wondered why it is so hard to make progress in your own spiritual growth? Satan is fighting desperately to stop any and all advances of the Kingdom of God. Satan's barrage has resulted in intensive spiritual warfare that has left many Christians dazzled and confused. How should we respond? We must learn more to win the battle. Paul reminds us,

"Though we live in the world, we do not wage war as the world does. The weapons we fight with are not the weapons of the world. On the contrary, they have divine power to demolish strongholds"(2 Cor. 10:3-4).

The human weapons of the flesh/world are useless against spiritual forces.  Only heavenly resources are able to deal with the real battle, the destruction of spiritual fortresses of evil.  By God's help, we are to overcome the world and its spiritual forces.

Some Christians give little evidence that they are in a life-and-death spiritual struggle of cosmic proportions.  We should recognize that *"our struggle is not against flesh and blood, but against the rulers, against the authorities, against the powers of the dark world and against the spiritual forces of evil in the heavenly realm"*(Eph. 6:12).

1.  *How do you react to the statement that there are "powers of the dark world" which are a force against everything that Christians try to do?*

2.  *John writes that "the whole world is under the control of the evil one"(1 John 5:19).  How is the evil giant  - the devil — defeated?*

Jesus Christ defeated Satan on the Cross.  This was God's plan to save us from Satan's slavery.  When Jesus said, "It is finished," He showed that the devil is defeated.  To avoid the devil, we must "come near to God and He will come near to you"(James 4:8).  The devil cannot beat us, for "the One who is in you is greater than the one who is in the world"(1 John 4:4).

Ephesians 6:10-11,13-18 informs us how to win over every difficulty and temptation that the devil puts before us.  The left hand column below contains the verses and the right hand

**WEEK EIGHT**                                      **151**

column describes armor we need to fight our battle against Satan: *"Be strong in the Lord and in his mighty power. Put on the full armor of God so that you can take your stand against the devil's schemes...put on the full armor of God, so that when the day of evil comes, you may be able to stand your ground, and, after you have done everything, to stand. Stand firm then,*

| | |
|---|---|
| *with the **belt of truth** buckled around your waist,* | The truth of the Bible is your belt. It "holds" your armor securely in place. |
| *with the **breastplate of righteousness** in place,* | The righteousness of Christ is your breastplate. With it, your heart will be protected from Satan's lies that you are not good enough for God. |
| *and with your **feet fitted** with the readiness that comes from the **Gospel of peace**.* | The Word equips you to be ready to move out to spread the Gospel of peace. Your feet are to be ready to move. |
| *In addition to all this, pick up the **shield of faith**, with which you can extinguish all the flaming arrows of the evil one.* | Faith is your shield to protect you from the devil. He will shoot all manner of problems and difficulties at you for the purpose of destroying your faith. |
| *Take the **helmet of salvation*** | Salvation is your helmet (more than a hat or cap), protecting your mind from Satan's lies. |
| *and the **sword of the Spirit**, which is the Word of God,* | The Word of God is an offensive weapon, a sword of the Holy Spirit. With it you can fight off Satan's lies. |

| *and **pray** in the Spirit on all occasions, with all kinds of prayers and requests. With this in mind, be alert and always keep on praying for all the saints."* | Pray to make your requests known to God. Our communication link is with the divine headquarters where we can request help for our battles. |
| --- | --- |

This "Spiritual Travel Guide" leads you to places in the Scriptures where you can examine the whole armor of God, which is made available to you for daily battles, so that you are dressed for war.

If we do not use these weapons, we have no hope of winning, for there is no other way to fight our spiritual battles successfully. All of the weapons are defensive ones except for the sword of the Spirit - the Word of God. There are no friendly discussions with the devil, for this is a conflict to the death between two fundamentally opposite views of truth and reality. There can be no truce in the name of Christian love.

Our first task then as a church is not to get ourselves comfortable and satisfied by keeping within the safety of the church walls. The battle is in our homes, at work, in recreation, and during social hours. We do not take on the full armor of God to play games.

*How have you seen Satan's attacks in your life?  How have you battled back?*

This is war, and a call to arms. We cannot fight the spiritual war without training or weapons. We cannot remain in the bunkhouse and refuse to answer calls to meals, exercise, and maneuvers in order to prepare for fighting effectively. "Take your

**WEEK EIGHT**                                     **153**

stand" (Eph. 6:11) is a phrase which belongs to the language of war against the powers of this dark world and the spiritual forces of evil in the heavenly realms.

This battle exists because we live in two worlds, two systems of government with two rulers: one in which "...you used to live when you followed the ways of this world and of the ruler of the kingdom of the air" and the other, "...because of His great love for us...God made us alive with Christ...and raised us up with Christ and seated us with Him in the heavenly realms..."(Eph. 2:2-6).

This battle is between the kingdom of light and the dominion of darkness (Col. 1:10-13)". It is between the pattern of this world and the will of God (Rom. 12:2), battling for our mind and heart. Citizenship in God's kingdom automatically brings with it a declaration of war from the devil and the world.

*What do these verses say about how the world views Christians?*

| | |
|---|---|
| John 15:18-21 | |
| 1 John 3:12-13 | |
| 2 Timothy 3:12 | |

Our job then is to be fully prepared for a life-long battle with the devil in spiritual warfare. This preparation means we must be willing to learn more about God and His plan for us. We are to understand our own weaknesses, those parts of our own personality that are most easily deceived by the lies that Satan whispers. Ask God to show you these areas and strengthen you for battle!

*What must you do to prepare properly for Satan's attack?*

**WEEK EIGHT**                                                       **154**

Go to God in prayer and ask Him to make you fully aware of the tactics the devil is using on you in spiritual warfare. After your time of prayer, spend a minute in silence. Record any thoughts you may have below.

## Day Two -- Communicating with God Through Prayer

Prayer is a vital activity for victory in spiritual warfare. As God speaks to us in His word, we speak to Him through prayer. Prayer is the breath of life through the Word to sustain our faith.

Our time with God spent in prayer allows us to communicate with God and for Him to communicate to us. Prayer is a personal communion or a person-to-person relationship with God. We pray to God for our own sake, for He does not need our prayers. We need this fellowship with God.

Prayer begins with retreating from the daily grind and activities. We need regular times of prayer for our relationship with Jesus to develop. It is through times of close fellowship with God that we learn how to pray and how to listen to God's voice through Scripture and as He speaks to our inner being.

*Describe your current habits for prayer and meditation on the Word of God. How does the time you spend with God compare with other activities in your life? How can you spend more time with God?*

God is not far away. He lives in Christians, and ministers to your inner being or spirit through the Holy Spirit.

The closeness of God is something in which we can take great comfort. Just as it takes time to develop relationships with other people, we must spend time with God to develop our relationship with Him.

We may live in close proximity to many other people without ever taking the time to know them. Have you ever had this experience with your neighbors? In the same way, we can fail to spend time with God even though He is very close to us and very willing to spend time with us. This can result in our feeling that God is a far away, distant and uncaring God. The farther we are from God, the easier it becomes for Satan's lies to trick us.

*What do the following verses tell you about prayer?*

| Luke 11:1 | |
|---|---|
| John 14:13-14 | |
| Hebrews 7:25 | |
| James 1:5-6 | |
| James 4:3 | |
| John 15:5-7 | |

What we pray for should be tied to our God-given purposes in life, not for self-interests. Prayer is to help fulfill our ministry for God, not to enlarge our own kingdom.

Jesus certainly wants us to ask for earthly things. In the Lord's Prayer. He teaches us to pray, "Give us this day our daily bread." However, He also teaches us, "Your will be done on earth as it is in heaven." So we make these requests acknowledging that they will be granted on His terms.

**WEEK EIGHT**                                    **156**

Many Christians use a pattern of prayer to help them keep a proper perspective, especially on the things for which they are asking. This pattern is: Adoration, Confession, Thanksgiving, and Supplication. Memorize these four points (ACTS), and use them in your prayer time:

ADORATION - Our specific words of praise reveal awe and respect.

Many of the Psalms are great words of praise. *"Praise Him for His acts of power, praise Him for His surpassing greatness"*(Ps. 150:2). If you find yourself lacking words of praise read Psalms 144-150. Concentrating on His majesty, holiness, and greatness in prayer removes us from earthly influences and distractions. As we acknowledge God's greatness, we see that nothing is too big for our great God to handle.

CONFESSION - During this time we acknowledge our sins, weaknesses, and failures.

Confession includes genuine sorrow for our sin, and admission of wrong against God and others. Confession means recognition of helplessness to correct the wrong and a plea for mercy for Jesus' sake. *"If we confess our sins, He is faithful and just and will forgive our sins and purify us from all unrighteousness"* (1 John 1:9).

Confession means that we desire to be strengthened by God to turn away from our sin. Sometimes we need God to show us our sins. Read Psalm 139:23-24. By asking God to show us our sins we give Him a chance to correct our thinking before we begin to make our petitions to Him. Many times as we confess our sins improper motives for our requests of God are exposed.

THANKSGIVING - We thank God for all the spiritual, material, and physical blessings He has given us: *"Give thanks in all circumstances, for this is God's will for you in Christ Jesus"* (I Thes. 15:8).

**WEEK EIGHT** **157**

We say "thank you" to Jesus for supplying our real needs, for protecting us from destructive evil, for praying for us, and for loving us enough to give us salvation and the Holy Spirit so that we may live pleasing to Him. Once again we grow in our understanding of our true position as redeemed, blessed, loved children of God. This puts a whole new light on what we pray for during the supplication time.

SUPPLICATION - We make requests for our own specific needs: "Do not be anxious about anything, but in everything by prayer and petition, with thanksgiving, present your requests to God" (Phil. 4:6).

We tell God the needs of our own family, friends, neighbors, community, and the entire world: We pray especially for those who do not know the love of Christ. "I urge, then, first of all, that requests, prayers, intercession and thanksgiving be made for everyone"(1 Tim. 2:1).

The ACTS format is not some rigid structure that must be followed each time you pray. It will, however, remind you of four major areas of prayer. The order gives us a clear picture of priority. We also see this priority in the Lord's Prayer which we will study next.

The Holy Spirit helps us to know our weaknesses and for what we ought to pray: "In the same way, the Spirit helps us in our weakness. We do not know what we ought to pray for, but the Spirit Himself intercedes for us with groans that words cannot express. And He who searches our hearts knows the mind of the Spirit, because the Spirit intercedes for the saints in accordance to God's will"(Rom. 8:26-27).

*Please write a prayer with one sentence for Adoration, Confession, Thanksgiving, Supplication (ACTS).*

God always answers prayers.  Sometimes He says "yes," sometimes "no," and sometimes "wait."  He knows best and sometimes makes us wait for a short or a long time.  He always wants the best for us.  He wants us to experience the victory Christ won for us.  But our ideas of what's best are many times different from God's plan.  Part of our victory in Christ is learning to wait on God's answers to our prayers.  Many times, other Christians will be a source of good counsel when we are waiting for answers to prayers.

1. *When has God answered your prayers with a yes? No? Wait? Do you struggle with waiting on God's answer to prayer? If so, how?*




2. *What elements of ACTS prayer do you need to emphasize in your prayer life?*




A regular time of prayer is important for you as a growing Christian.  If you have not already developed this habit, go to God and ask Him to help you develop it.

**Day Three -- The Lord's Prayer**

The tone and content of the Lord's Prayer reveals the spiritual emphasis of a Christian's life.  We can learn much about how we should pray by looking closely at the Lord's Prayer. *"This, then, is how you should pray: Our Father in heaven, hallowed be your name, your kingdom come, your will be done*

**WEEK EIGHT**                                          **159**

*on earth as it is in heaven. Give us today our daily bread. Forgive us our debts, as we also have forgiven our debtors. And lead us not into temptation, but deliver us from the evil one"* (Matt. 6:9-13).

In the Seven Petitions, only one asks for material possessions; all the rest are spiritual. We are encouraged to pray "Our Father" instead of "my Father," since we pray for the whole body of Christ and for fellow Christians, not just simply for our own needs. This reminds us that as Christians we are connected to others as well as God. This prayer shows the constant consideration of others. In Christ's name, we go boldly to God's throne of mercy and grace.

**The First Petition - "Hallowed be Your Name."**

The prayer begins in adoration. The word "Hallowed" means holy or revered. We are recognizing His holiness and greatness. We are asking God to help us to keep His name holy. God's name stands for everything He is and does in His purity. We keep His name holy, by not taking His name in vain. Most importantly we hold to His Word faithfully and live lives that honor God.

*How do we keep God's name holy?*

**The Second Petition  - "Your Kingdom Come."**

God's rule of grace through Jesus is called His Kingdom - the Kingdom which includes all who believe in Jesus. God's kingdom has come to the world, but here we pray that it will be a reality in the life of His church and in our lives. We ask God to rule over us now and come in glory as our King to rule over us forever in heaven.

*How does God use us to bring His kingdom to others?*


**The Third Petition** - "Your Will be Done on Earth as it is in Heaven."

God's will includes all He wants to do for us, and what He wants us to do for Him. This may also include testing and strengthening our faith through suffering. We ask God to help us believe that He, as our dear Father, wants only what is best for us.

*How can we tell if something is our will, the devil's will, or God's will?*


**The Fourth Petition** - "Give us this Day our Daily Bread."

"Daily bread" means our food and everything else we need for our physical life. We ask God for our own needs and those of other people. We should not worry, for our heavenly Father is our provider. We should be satisfied with what He gives and show thanks. This is a prayer that God should supply our needs. It is the only supplication request in the prayer that deals with physical things.

*How can we avoid taking our daily bread for granted, or complaining about it, or wasting it?*


**WEEK EIGHT** 

**The Fifth Petition** - "Forgive us our Debts as we also have forgiven our Debtors."

In this prayer, we confess all our sins to God, even those which are not known by us. We need God's forgiveness every day. We place ourselves on God's mercy and ask Him to forgive us. We can pray with complete confidence as we come with repentant hearts. Our Father's forgiveness moves us to forgive other people fully and freely when they sin against us. This is serious business because we ask God to forgive us as we forgive others.

1. *If God has already forgiven all our sins, why do we keep on praying for forgiveness of our sins?*

2. *How does the Fifth Petition emphasize that we must forgive others?*

**The Sixth Petition** - "And Lead us not into Temptation."

An accurate translation of this prayer is, "Don't allow us to be tempted." God tempts no one to sin, but here we ask God to watch over us so that the devil, the world, and our sinful self may not deceive us or draw us into any sin. God's enemies tempt us to draw us away from God, but God uses it to bring us closer to Him. We need our heavenly Father's help daily.

*"If you play with fire, you will get your fingers burnt." How does this apply to facing temptations?*

**WEEK EIGHT** 162

**The Seventh Petition** - "But Deliver us from Evil."

Our request is to spare us from trouble, according to His will, and help us bear any trouble patiently and take it away from us soon. We ask for God's grace to protect us from evil while here on earth. Our Father will set us free from all evil forever when He takes us home to Himself in heaven.

*What evils and situations are you focused on when you ask God to deliver you from evil?*

**The  Doxology** - "For Yours is the Kingdom, and the Power, and the Glory forever and ever. AMEN" Our God is the all-powerful Lord of heaven and earth. He is worthy of all glory as the God of our salvation. AMEN means: Yes, it shall be so.

*Are you confident and sure that God hears and answers your prayers?  Why or why not?*

We have spent the last two days reviewing some important concepts about prayer. Have you established a special time and place to go to God in prayer? Consider the following as you establish your daily routine of spending time with God:

- Are you a morning or night person? Experiment to find the best time of day for you to pray. Your goal is to add a new habit to your life. It may be difficult at first. Remember Satan does not want you to spend time with your heavenly Father.

- What changes do you need to make in your schedule to allow time with God?  Will you have to get up earlier in the morning?  Will you have to rearrange your evening habits?
- What might interrupt your time with God?  Minimize interruptions by telling the people you live with that you need this time with God and you don't want to be disturbed unless it's an emergency.

Go to God in prayer and ask Him to guide you in establishing your prayer habit and time with Him daily.  After your time of prayer, spend a minute in silence.  Record any thoughts you might have below.


## Day Four -- The Devil's Barriers and Tricks

Our evil adversary is spiritual: Satan - the serpent (Genesis 3:5), the devil - our  adversary (1 Peters 5:8).  He works through our own sinful flesh (Romans 7:23), worldly lusts (1 Peter 2:11), and the system of this world (John 16:33).

**The devil is a most powerful enemy.  The following Scripture passages identify some of Satan's tactics and His supernatural power.**

| | |
|---|---|
| 2 Tim. 2:26 | He takes people captive |
| 2 Cor. 4:4 | He has the ability to blind people's minds |
| Job 1:7 | Yet he has limitations, for he is neither all-powerful nor all-knowing |
| Acts 15:24 | He raises questions to confuse us and makes promises to mislead us |
| Matt. 7:15 | He works especially through false teachers and false religious systems: "...They come to you in  sheep's  clothing,  but  inwardly  they  are |

| | ferocious wolves" |
|---|---|
| Luke 10:17,20 | Satan has a multitude of helpers called demons or evil spirits |
| Luke 8:30 | Demons may assume personal names like Legion |
| Luke 4:33-35, 41; 8:28-30 | Demons may use intelligent speech |
| Mark 1:23-24; Acts 16:16-17 | Demons recognized the identity of Christ and Paul |
| 2 Cor. 11:14; Rev. 9:7-10, 17 | Satan or his demons appear and may look as though they are angels of light or as hideous and fearsome beings |
| Eph. 2:1-2; Daniel 10:13,20; John 12:31; 2 Thes. 2:8-10 | Satan and his evil angels seek to control people and political governments and the whole world's philosophy and course of history |

Satan and his demons openly attack God's purposes. They attempt to oppress humanity. They confront especially believers in Christ. When Peter tempted Christ, Christ said, "Get behind Me, Satan." The persecuting Jews hindered Paul from coming to the Thessalonians, and Paul said, "Satan tempted me." When covetousness motivated Ananias to lie, Peter said, "Why has Satan filled your heart?" He even seeks to validate his deceit by the use of Scriptures and quoting God (Matthew 4:3-11; Genesis 3:1 - "....has God said").

The chief characteristic of demonic influence and possession is a distinct "other" personality within. The demons have a longing for a body to possess (Matthew 8:31). They converse through the organs of speech, and give evidence of personality, desire and fear. The demon changes entirely the moral character of those he enters, compelling them to act contrary to their normal behavior.

A demon may speak using the voice of the possessed person. Sometimes they have knowledge of supernatural realities (Luke 4:33-35; 8:26-29). A person may show supernatural strength (Acts 19:16). Demons may cause a person to have seizures and other physical problems (Matthew 17:14-21).

Christians should seek to destroy the enemy's strongholds. Satan is bound through the Word of Jesus and by His blood. Satan cannot tolerate Jesus being confessed as the divine Redeemer. There is no greater power against demons than the blood of Jesus. Prayer is also a mighty force against the Evil One. Our victory is assured and secured by Christ.

1. *What evidence is there that the devil is doing his work in our community?*

2. *How does the devil disguise himself as an angel of light in churches?*

3. *How does the devil hinder the advance of the Gospel and oppose Christ's mission?*

**WEEK EIGHT**  166

The will of Satan is defeated through the Incarnation of Christ, who came as the Divine Invader to destroy what the devil does (1 John 3:8). Jesus clearly viewed His mission as including a campaign against evil forces for the sake of liberating people from the devil and demons.

*1.*    *On the basis of Eph. 6:10-19, how is the power of Satan and the demons curbed and stopped?*

*2.*    *How does Satan attack you?   What areas of your personality allow you to be tempted and result in sinful behavior?*

2 Corinthians 10:4-5 shows us we must be ready to resist sin in our lives: *"The weapons we fight with are not the weapons of the world. On the contrary, they have divine power to demolish strongholds. We demolish arguments and every pretension that sets itself up against the knowledge of God, and we take captive every thought to make it obedient to Christ."*

Go to God in prayer and ask Him not to allow Satan to exploit our weaknesses or put barriers between Him and us, and that any unforgiven hurt, bad habits or deeply ingrained attitudes to our past will be healed by His grace. After your time of prayer, spend a minute in silence. Record any thoughts you might have below.

## Day Five -- My Ministering Angels

Angels are popular these days. Have you seen rows of books about them at the bookstores? The television shows? There are many dangers in the popular thoughts about angels. The difficulty in much of what we see today is angel worship. Worshipping angels instead of the creator of angels is prohibited. God says that we should have no other gods before Him.

The following verse shows that people who worship angels are unspiritual, filled with idle notions, unconnected with Christ, the Head and unable to grow. We are also warned to beware of these people. *"Do not let anyone who delights in false humility and the worship of angels disqualify you for the prize. Such a person goes into great detail about what he has seen, and his unspiritual mind puffs him up with idle notions. He has lost connection with the Head, from whom the whole body, supported and held together by its ligaments and sinews, grows as God causes it to grow"(Col. 2:18-19).*

When the apostle John was given a vision as recorded in the Book of Revelation, he tried to bow down and worship the angels he encountered. They very sternly rebuked him and said, "Do not do it! I am a fellow servant with you and with your brothers the prophets and of all who keep the words of this book. Worship God!" (Rev. 22:9).

Do these passages describe anyone you know? We need to develop a proper understanding of angels. First, God has given us His helpers, the holy angels, to minister to us and to fight against the devil and his tricks. Ministering angels serve all believers in their calling and work (Psalm 91:11-12). Luke 16:22 tells about the angels escorting the soul of a believer to heaven.

What are angels? They are spirits sent to serve those who receive salvation (Hebrews 1:14). The good angels are numerous and very strong; they carry out God's commands, and praise God (Psalm 103:20-21).

Angels worship before the throne of God and serve Him obediently (Psalm 148:2; Hebrews 1:6). They celebrate before the throne of God when sinners repent (Luke 15:10). Acts 12:23 tells about angels who were commissioned to administer divine judgment upon Herod.

We have great comfort in the fact that God has sent His holy angels as guardians. Whatever our need, problems, or challenges, these ministering angels will help bring God's protection and blessings for us. Knowing this, Christians will take advantage of the protective force God has given them, praying daily that God's holy angels will care for them. We do not focus our worship on angels above God.

1. *What do good angels do?*


2. *How did angels serve believers in*

- *Exodus 14:19?*


- *Daniel 6:22?*


- *Acts 12:7?*

**WEEK EIGHT**

3. *What good news do Psalm 91:11 and Hebrews 1:14 tell us? How does the Hebrews passage differ from the world's view of angels?*


**Major Points to Review**
1. *Satan is fighting desperately to stop your spiritual growth. How are you prepared for the battle?*


2. *Prayer is an important part of our daily battle against Satan and sin. What area of your prayer life needs to be improved so that you are strengthened for battle?*


3. *Satan and his demons are powerful enemies that employ many strategies to tear us down and limit the growth of our faith. What is Satan's favorite tactic to separate you from God or to wear you down?*


4. *How has your understanding of angels changed after this study?*


**WEEK EIGHT**

**OBSERVATIONS/REFLECTIONS ON WHAT YOU STUDIED THIS WEEK:**

1.  What matters or issues would you like to know more about?  What, if anything, troubled you about what you studied?

2.  How has your faith grown or been modified?

3.  What new knowledge or insights have you learned?

4.  How will this affect your life?

**WEEK EIGHT** 171

# WEEK NINE

# LIVING FOR CHRIST

## Day One -- Freedom in Christ -- No Slaveries

The world has a definition of freedom that emphasizes our choices. After all, American freedom is to pursue life, liberty and the pursuit of happiness, right? It is that very freedom that allows us to worship God without persecution. Unfortunately, this freedom can also be destructive. We can choose drink too much, eat to much or pursue our desires to the point that it negatively affects us and those around us. Sometimes in our freedom to pursue happiness we become addicted or enslaved to the very things we thought would bring happiness.

*What do we learn about freedom in Romans 8:21? As you consider this verse, what is the danger of being a slave to anything or anyone?*

God has a different idea of freedom. God's idea of freedom is that we have the ability to say "no." We can live a life of self-control, not letting anything, other than our relationship with God become a requirement. This relationship strengthens our ability to be self-controlled and motivates us to do positive, constructive things that build up God's kingdom. Such activity is not a requirement, but a response to God's love for us.

*What does it mean that our service to God is not under the Law, but under grace?  How can we experience freedom in Christ and yet be obedient to His will?*

To have freedom means that we are not under the power of anything or anyone but Christ.  It means that our conscience is not answerable ultimately to human authority, but to God.  But it also means that every area of our lives should be under the Lordship of Christ, who sets us free from all human slavery.  Not only the freedom, but also the strength to maintain that freedom, comes from Jesus Christ.

*What do the following passages say about freedom in Christ?*

| | |
|---|---|
| Col. 2:6-23 What are the hollow and deceptive philosophies of the world? Why do they lack value? | |
| Col. 3:1-4:6 What is different about the rules given here and the world's rules? | |

Freedom means many things to many people: freedom to a philosopher may mean manipulation through wisdom; to the poor, wealth; to the student, the three o'clock bell; and to the convict, escape from prison.  In all these cases, the person is thinking like a slave.

*What are some of the forces hindering us from being truly free?*

**Week Nine**                                    173

Jesus gives us another kind of freedom which is available to all people, and yet so few people claim or possess it. His is freedom from the slavery of sin, and from rules and regulations for earning His acceptance.

Man's freedom, lost in the Fall, is restored in redemption and experienced in the process of sanctification (living for Christ). In Christ, Christians are delivered from the bondage of the human will, now free to do God's will. Jesus said, "I tell you the truth, everyone who sins is a slave to sin. Now a slave has no permanent place in the family, but a son belongs to it forever. So if the Son sets you free, you will be free indeed"(John 8:34-36).

The heart of the Gospel is the freedom from the need to keep the Law in order to earn salvation.

Christian freedom from bondage to sin means to be released from whatever prison is holding us, from whatever is binding us spiritually, mentally, and emotionally. Freedom in Christ frees us from pride, resentment, jealousies, fears and obsessions which may be eating away at us.

*How may you find yourself in a situation of being in any prison of sin?*

Church rules which invade or intrude upon Christian freedom tend to create a rash of contradictions and hypocrisies, for they cater to craving for acceptance by human standards and efforts. For example, Jesus gave severe warnings against drunkenness, but not against drinking. What Jesus taught was an internal discipline which controls external forces. His love and grace are the strengths for the freedom He gives us.

*1. What is the truth about freedom in John. 8:31-32? What is involved in being free from all slaveries?*

**Week Nine**

*2. What is the difference between freedom and lawlessness(breaking any laws we don't like)?*


Go to God in prayer and ask Him to confront things that may tempt or enslave you.   After your time of prayer, spend a minute in silence.  Record any thoughts you might have below.


## Day Two -- New Steps to Contentment and Happiness

*Please finish this sentence: I would only be happy if:*


We all seek the answer to this question.  Sometimes, we think we have found it in some earthly thing, only to be disappointed.  Only God knows what will bring us contentment and happiness in life.  His plan allows for us:
- To be loved
- To be forgiven
- Have a clear concept of self
- Understand our purpose in life
- Have eternal security
- Have hope for the future

These are deep, yearning emotional and spiritual needs we all have in common. We are all created this way by God who alone can fill these needs.  People cannot satisfy them.  No person has enough love, forgiveness, resources or hope to share with us in the amount that we need.  Nor can we find lasting satisfaction in the pleasures of this world, even though many try.  Only God can fill the emptiness of our heart by fellowship with Him.

*How has God filled the emptiness of your heart?  Are there empty places that you have yet to let Him fill?*


Created as social beings, another need is to be related satisfactorily to people and to God.  We may remain lonely no matter how many friends are around us, if we are not related intimately to Jesus Christ.  Our own sin will interfere with our relationship to others and God, creating even deeper longings. Correcting sinful behavior in our lives becomes important if we expect these relationships to grow.

The first step in this process is to recognize damaging sinful behaviors in your life.  Many people are afraid to open themselves to God and to others. They know something is missing, but are afraid to abandon behaviors they have used to bring even temporary happiness and comfort.  Openness is necessary if we are to be honest in our responsibility for choosing and defining our lives.  The real questions are:

- "What do we really want out of life - momentary pleasures or God's long-lasting satisfaction?
- What I am I willing to give up in order to experience the contentment and happiness God desires for me (delayed gratification)?
- Am I willing to exercise God's plan for my freedom from sin?"

There are many habits and cravings which hamper us in our spiritual life and growth which can only be resolved by taking the proper spiritual steps.  Sometimes we deny problems exist.

**Week Nine**                                                              176

We may try to cover-up the problem, rationalize or simply avoid the subject altogether. Guilt, shame and remorse may consume us. Alienation or separation may result as those close to us push for a solution. In all cases, the longer we deny the existence of things in our lives that keep us from growing spiritually, the more difficult it becomes to address those issues.

Today, many things have become addictive or compulsive agents on which excessive dependency for contentment and happiness has been built. Are you aware of any the following addictions or compulsions in yourself?

- Alcohol
- Drugs (including cigarettes and caffeine)
- Obsessive work, achievement and success
- Food compulsions (including soft drinks)
- Control obsessions , especially in personal and family relationships.
- Approval dependency (the need to please people)
- Gossiping (tearing others down in order to build up self)
- Busyness (proving our goodness as parents, spouses, employees - no time for God)
- Money compulsions (overspending, gambling, hoarding)
- Materialism (perfect house, cars, vacations)
- Sexual addictions, including the use of pornography
- Co-dependency (the need to have other people dependent on you or you upon them)
- Religious legalism (preoccupation with the rituals, form, rules and regulations of religion rather than the spiritual relationship in Christ)
- Perfectionism
- Organizing or structuring obsessively (the need to have everything perfectly in place every moment)
- Excessive cleaning

**Week Nine**                                              177

- Excessive exercise and physical conditioning
- Imagined physical illnesses (hypochondria)
- Compulsion to cosmetics (even cosmetic surgery)

These are dysfunctions, illnesses and sins which affect our body, mind and spirit. They make us unable to control ourselves so that we actually lose the mastery of our lives. They cause us to try to control others and to avoid admitting our own problems and guilt.

God alone can heal us through Jesus Christ, our Savior and Lord. Taking away all pretense, excuses, and denial, we must be fully prepared to turn from our sinful habits, receive the forgiveness of Christ, and experience the contentment and happiness God alone can give.

***Why is it difficult to admit our weaknesses?***

Our addictions, compulsions, obsessions or sinful habits, whatever they may be, may be a symptom of the real problem - an outer expression of an inner spiritual weakness or illness. Have you ever found yourself justifying a negative sinful behavior as a reward you give yourself? Many times we experience disappointments induced by the actions of others and then use the situation to justify our sinful behavior. We will continue to be driven compulsively until we deal with the real spiritual issue. Our position as forgiven children of God is the spiritual issue. Instead of facing this issue and dealing with our behaviors, we deny there is anything wrong. Through denial, we can rationalize and trick ourselves into thinking we are not exactly giving up our values, or that we are not really sinning.

**Week Nine**                                                    **178**

*Paul and Peter urged a life of self-control. What do the following verse say about self-control?*

| 2 Cor. 10:5 | |
|---|---|
| Gal. 5:22-23 | |
| 2 Peter 1:5-6 | |

A life out of control, where indulgences are rampant, is not a life of freedom, but a life of chaos and slavery. We need to commit ourselves to a life of wholeness that is empowered not by us but by the Holy Spirit through God's Word and prayer.

*Why is it vital for overcoming any problem of compulsion/obsession/ addiction to make up our minds that change and then control of these sins are the most important thing in our life?*

*Are you ready to follow these steps if you have a sinful habit that needs change?*

1.  **Give up control - admit you are weak. You are powerless over your habits, compulsions and addictions. You must admit that you cannot manage or control your life by yourself.**
2.  **Look to God, your only hope for change or recovery. The Holy Spirit has caused you to believe that only a Power greater than yourself (the Triune God, Father Son and Holy Spirit) can change you and restore you to stability. Only Jesus can lead you to fullness of life.**
3.  **Change direction, turn away from your sinful behavior to God. You make this decision by the Spirit, turning your will and life over to the care of God through forgiveness in Jesus Christ as manager of your life.**

4. **Honestly look at yourself.** Have you made a searching and fearless moral inventory to assess your strengths and weaknesses?

5. **Begin healing and reconciliation** by admitting to God, to yourself and to someone else the exact nature of your wrongs.

6. **Stop holding on.** You have repented and are ready to have God remove all these defects of character and give you healing through Christ.

7. **Be ready to make necessary changes in your life style.** Humbly ask God to remove your sins and forgive you through Jesus, renewing your mind and transforming your life.

8. **Restore relationships.** Make a list of people you have harmed. Be willing to make amends to them all.

9. **Reconcile and build bridges to others.** Make direct amends to people you have harmed wherever possible, except when it would do harm.

10. **Keep on the road to abundant living.** Continue to take personal inventory and promptly admit when you are wrong.

11. **Maintain spiritual health and strength.** Through prayer and meditation on God's Word strengthen your contact with Him. Pray for knowledge of His will for you and the power of the Holy Spirit to accomplish it.

12. **Live and share these truths.** Share Christ's healing and freeing message of love with those still in slavery and addicted (whether to great or small things), and to practice these principles as the Holy Spirit leads and empowers.

Our Christian faith will no longer be a bunch of disconnected Bible facts, but it will be an integrated understanding of God's Word connected as the Way, the Truth and the Life (John 14:6).  This is the way we will have true happiness and security which nothing can destroy.

*How can we as a church help people who are having struggles with sinful habits?*

Go to God in prayer and ask Him for help to follow these principles for growth.  After your time of prayer, spend a minute in silence.  Record any thoughts you might have below.

## Day Three -- No Promise of Heaven on Earth

Living for Christ will not drive away problems and suffering.  People who feel God should reward their good intentions and service with a conflict-free life often ask, "Why would God allow this to happen to me?...How could a loving God allow such suffering to exist?...Why me, God?"

*When was the last time you questioned God about a difficulty you were experiencing?*

Living for God is not a deposit on a trouble-free life.  The sin of Adam and Eve brought pain and death into the world and into our lives, and we feel the consequences (Gen. 3:16-19).  Human sinfulness causes much suffering, such as injustice and war, which harm many uninvolved people.

**Week Nine**                                                      181

A popular notion among some Christians today is that God will deliver his people from all pain, illness, suffering, relational difficulties and financial problems.  Look at the disciple's lives after Jesus' ascension into heaven.  Did they experience problems?   To be sure, God has delivered us from sin and hell through Jesus' death and resurrection.  However, sin has consequence.  As long as we live in a sinful world we will experience the negative consequences of sin to some degree.  Sometimes sin just nags creating the ordinary daily frustration.  Other time it hurls us to the outer limits of our endurance.  In any case, God can work good out of our situation.  His healing love is the secret to facing all struggle.

The suffering of Jesus is an example for believers, providing a right perspective on the meaning of suffering: "To this you were called, because Christ suffered for you, leaving you an example, that you should follow in His steps"(2 Peter 2:29).

*Describe a time of difficulty or suffering you have experienced in each of the following areas:*
**Because of your own sin:**


**Because of the sin of others:**


**Because of sin in the world (sickness, natural disaster):**


**Because you are a Christian:**


**Has any good come of these difficulties?  Why or why not?**

Following Jesus' example, we surrender ourselves to the will of God (Matthew 26:39). By God's grace, our suffering gives much good for serving God: "...We also rejoice in our sufferings, because we know that suffering produces perseverance; perseverance, character; and character, hope"(Romans 5:3-4).

James 1:2-4 shows the value of trials and testing of our faith, as it produces endurance, maturity, and wholeness. Paul told how his prison chains were part of God's plan to advance the Gospel, as he encouraged others (Phil.1:12-14).

John 15's message that Jesus is the Vine and we are the branches reveals God's use of problems and trials in our lives: "He cuts off every branch in Me that bears no fruit, while every branch that does bear fruit He prunes so that it may be even more fruitful...This is to My Father's glory, that you bear much fruit, showing yourselves to be My disciples"(John. 15:2,8). God's pruning process through suffering is to make us more fruitful and to enlarge our service to God. It makes us more mature in our faith (1 Peter 1:6-7). God's purpose is not to give us pain, but lovingly to make us His faithful servants and to guide us on productive paths.

*Examine the following Scripture passages for additional information on suffering:*

| | |
|---|---|
| The purpose of difficulties and problems in our lives - John 15:2, 8 | |
| The purpose of troubles - 1 Peter 1:6-7 | |

| The purpose of pain and discipline -- Hebrews 12:5, 11 | |
|---|---|
| A good thing that comes from suffering --1 Peter 5:10 | |
| How we are to act when we are troubled -- Romans 5:3-5 and 12:12 | |

From these passages, we can see a different response to suffering from Christians than from non-believers. We can only respond this way because of God's work in us through the power of the Holy Spirit. A question we should ask ourselves continually is, "How could God use my current circumstance as witness to the world?" We have many opportunities in suffering and adversity to show the world how different we are because of Christ. Are you ready to be this kind of witness?

Go to your Father in heaven now in prayer and ask Him to show you how He is using your circumstances for His glory and purpose. Ask for an extra measure of His grace so that your challenges will be a great witness to the world. After your time of prayer, spend a minute in silence. Record any thoughts you might have below.

## Day Four -- The Fruit of the Spirit

Our responses to the world require much more than we are capable of. Not only does God offer the power of the Holy Spirit, but He also gives the fruit of the Spirit. This fruit is what grows in us as a result of the Holy Spirit living and working in us.

*What are some of the character traits listed:*

| Eph. 4:1-3 | |
|---|---|
| 2 Peter 1:5-7 | |

These verses describe what God wants us to be like. We don't have to struggle for these expressions of our faith, for they are a gift of the Holy Spirit for which we are to pray.

*Why is it impossible to achieve any degree of love and peace without being attached directly to their source, Jesus Christ?*

We are given a long list of the fruit of the Spirit in Galatians 5:22-23: "The fruit of the Spirit is love, joy, peace, patience, kindness, goodness, faithfulness, gentleness, and self-control. Against such things there is no law." Let's look more closely at each trait.

## Love

The foundation for all fruit in our lives is love. Our ability to love comes from God's love for us. This is a much different type of love than the world talks about. Poems and songs about love express many emotions people feel, but they say very little about the real character of Christian love. Much of today's talk about love deals with the need to be loved and to love others for personal gain.

Romantic love and self-centered love pleads, "If you love me, you will do what I want." Biblical love says, "If you love me, you will respect my convictions and not push me into something which I consider wrong and do not want to do."

The English language uses one word, "love," to express all kinds of love, while the Greek language of the original New Testament uses basically four: **eros**, an emotional response to others' attractiveness, seeking to gain advantage for itself; **phileo**, responding to other's kindness, a companionship; **storge**, family affection; and **agape**, which flows freely to serve the needs of others without expectation of return. The latter describes God's love for humanity, and the love people should have for one another.

Christian love has a Christ-likeness about it, for we are told to "love... as Christ loved"(Eph. 5:2, 25). This is an individual and a community of believers' love. It speaks the truth with love (Eph. 4:15).

*1 Corinthians 13:4-8 tells what agape love is and what it is not.*

| | |
|---|---|
| *Love is:* | |
| *Love is not:* | |

We must grow in our understanding that Christian love is a verb. It is an action rather than a noun.


**Joy**

We are to rejoice always (1 Thes. 5:16; 4:4). Being happy is not enough. Joy is not limited by outside circumstances, for it endures in spite of bad conditions. We rejoice because our situation is good in God, grounded and secure in Jesus Christ.

186

**Week Nine**

## Peace

Peace with God refers to the condition when God is reconciled to us, so that we are not in conflict or rebellion against Him. This peace reflects the inner tranquillity which we have because Christ lives in us, and God is in charge. Peace with others is experienced because we have been forgiven by God, and we have the strength to forgive others.

Jesus tore down the wall of hostility that divides people. Jesus said, "Blessed are those who make peace"(Matthew 5:9). God has called us into peace in His body, where Christ's peace is to control us.

## Patience

Christian patience is calm determination to endure, a perseverance to live like a child of God. Patience is true love that tolerates frustration, and suffers mistreatment if need be. It does not respond wrongly to provocations, but tolerates the weaknesses of others (Col. 3:13).

## Kindness and Goodness

Kindness is love exercising compassion and forgiveness, while goodness is being gracious and generous. Both are love's service and behavior. Opportunities for doing good are almost unlimited, so we should never be tired of living the right way (Gal. 6:9).

## Faithfulness

Faithfulness is love keeping its promises and sticking to its commitments. It is reliability and loyalty with integrity. God is faithful in everything. So should we be.

**Gentleness**

Gentleness is love refusing to be harsh or demanding, even if it has a right to push its own interests. It shows respect for the rights of others.

**Self-control**

Self-control is love voluntarily stopping actions that may be harmful to ourselves or to others. Desires must be controlled, so that they do not exceed proper limits. We should insist on order in our lives through the help of God through His word.

1. *How is self-control as a fruit of the Spirit connected with the keeping of the First Commandment ("You shall have no other gods before Me)?*

2. *Why is it difficult for Christians to achieve the fourth type of love - agape love?*

Go to God in prayer and tell Him about any of the fruit of the Spirit in which you need to grow stronger and show more grace. After your time of prayer, spend a minute in silence. Record any thoughts you might have below.

## Day Five -- Living as Disciples of Christ

Someone has said, "God doesn't have little places...only right places." The right place for the Christian is to be on the road to discipleship. Discipleship describes the real journey of faith.

Satan will try to talk you out of taking this journey. He probably tells you lies regularly. Have you had thoughts like, "I'm just not good enough" or "I can never live up to these standards" or maybe "I've failed so many times before, what's the use?" Satan will raise a lot of questions and use a number of tricks to try to stop you from continuing on the discipleship road.

Take comfort that Jesus' disciples, like us, were very ordinary people with all the human faults and weaknesses which we have - sometimes fearful, selfish, impatient, argumentative, proud, weary, weak in faith, slow to learn and quick to forget.

All Christians are disciples, whether strong or weak. **A faithful disciple is a Christian who learns, grows, matures and shapes in the image of Jesus Christ, keeping strong in the Word to edify Christians and to evangelize non-Christians.** Jesus said that when a disciple is fully mature, he will be "like his teacher" (Luke 6:40).

*In order to grow spiritually healthy, the disciple must be willing to:*
1. Learn and be teachable.
2. Submit to authority and be quick to obey (1 Thes. 5:12; Hebrews 11:17; Luke 5:4-9).
3. Be trustworthy and faithful (1 Cor. 4:12; Mark 11:22).
4. Serve and be a servant (Matt. 20:26-28; John 13:17).
5. Be forgiving (Luke 17:14; Eph. 4:32; Col. 3:16).
6. Share faith with others, witnessing (John. 1:1-3; 1:8).
7. Adopt God's priorities (Matt. 6:33; Acts 6:2-4).
8. Rejoice in the Lord and have a joyful attitude (Phil. 4:4).

*1. Which of the traits of a disciple do you believe are most important? Which ones are indispensable?*

2. *What can we as individuals or as a group do to encourage other Christian disciples to seek the priorities which God desires in them?*

Our goal as Christian disciples is to become mature in faith (Eph. 4:14-15; Col. 1:28). Maturity in Christ is more than being active in church programs. It means showing love and witnessing in our relationships in our homes, leisure, work and community activities.

**There are barriers to faithful discipleship:**

- Failure to set priorities (Matthew 6:33)
- Slavery to things - stereo, computer, car, TV, videos, etc., (Luke 12:15)
- Pride (Romans 12:3)
- Escaping reality by drinking, doing drugs, etc. (Eph. 5:18)
- Selfishness (Luke 12:21)
- Obsession with money (Eccl. 5:10-11)
- Robbing God by poor giving (Malachi 3:8)
- A critical spirit (Matt. 7:1)
- Gossip and unbridled tongue (James 3:2)
- Infidelity and sex outside of marriage (1 Cor. 6:18ff.; Matt. 5:27-28)
- Envy (Prov. 14:30)
- Bad temper (Prov. 16:32)

God does not want you to feel defeated. Instead, He wants you to experience His love and grace. Bask in this love and grace until such time that you are ready to take the next step in your walk with Him.

*What attitude and conduct does God want in disciples?*

**Week Nine**                                   190

2 Peter 1:5-11 shows how we may reach God's goals as Christian disciples by taking steps to maturity to have a growing faith. *" For this very reason, make every effort to add to your faith goodness; and to goodness, knowledge; and to knowledge, self-control; and to self-control, perseverance; and to perseverance, godliness; and to godliness, brotherly kindness; and to brotherly kindness, love. For if you possess these qualities in increasing measure, they will keep you from being ineffective and unproductive in your knowledge of our Lord Jesus Christ. But if anyone does not have them, he is near-sighted and blind, and has forgotten that he has been cleansed from his past sins. Therefore, my brothers, be all the more eager to make your calling and election sure. For if you do these things, you will never fall, and you will receive a rich welcome into the eternal kingdom of our Lord and Savior Jesus Christ. "*

**How does Nahum 1:7 bring Gospel and encouragement to us in relation to seeking to live as faithful disciples?**

Go to God in prayer and thank him for making you one of His disciples, and ask Him to give you full understanding of how you can express your faith as a disciple. After your time of prayer, spend a minute in silence. Record any thoughts you might have below.

**Major Points to Review**

1. *What can you strengthen to enhance your Christian witness?*

**Week Nine**                                                               191

2. *On day two, we studied twelve principles to make us content and happy. How can you use these steps to assure your joy and happiness?*

3. *How does God use pain and suffering in our lives to strengthen us for our journey?*

4. *Can you write the fruit of the Spirit without looking at a list?*

5. *Give your definition of a disciple of Christ.*

**OBSERVATIONS/REFLECTIONS ON WHAT YOU STUDIED THIS WEEK:**

1. What matters or issues would you like to know more about? What, if anything, troubled you about what you studied?

2. What new knowledge or insights have you learned?

3. How has your faith grown or been modified?

4. How will this affect your life?

# WEEK TEN

# GOD GIVES US A SPECIAL ROAD MAP:

# THE TEN COMMANDMENTS

God gave the Ten Commandments to His people through Moses at Mount Sinai more than 3,000 years ago. They are still as relevant for life today as they were then. They have lasting significance, for God's character is unchangeable. These laws originate from our almighty God and from His eternal character; therefore, their moral value cannot change. The world is in desperate need to see the name and character of God modeled in the lives of Christians who still take His Word seriously.

*If you rated your witness to the world on the basis of your obedience to the Ten Commandments how would you score?*


These Commandments, when coupled with the teachings of Christ, are still the best guidelines for practical daily living known to man. By following them, we become living demonstrations to the world of God's power to work goodness in our hearts. This goodness has a powerful affect on those who do not believe.

The Ten Commandments reveal God's Law showing us our failure and rebellion. We see His love in giving His Commandments as protection from harming ourselves and others, and as freedom from slavery.  God cared enough to give the Commandments both as a danger signal and as a guide for Christian conduct.  Their true function is to lead us to a life of holiness by His grace.

These commands and guidelines were intended to direct the community of believers to meet the needs of each individual in a loving and responsible manner.  By Jesus' time, however, most people looked at the Law the wrong way.  They saw it as a means of prospering and gaining acceptance from God and from man. They thought that obedience was the way to earn God's protection from foreign invasion and natural disasters.  Law-keeping became an end in itself, not the means to fulfill God's ultimate law of love. A proper understanding of the Ten Commandments will help us avoid the same mistake.

## Day One -- The Ten Commandments as a Blessing and Grace Event

We can see the love of God as He makes a covenant and promise with these words, *"I am making a covenant with you. Before all your people I will do wonders never before done in any nation in all the world. The people you live among will see how awesome is the work that I, the LORD, will do for you. Obey what I command you today.  I will drive out before you...(your enemies)"* (Ex. 74:10-11).

***What is the good news according to this passage?***

The Ten Commandments should not take the freedom out of life, but help give stability and orderliness. They give positive direction to Christian faith that can spare us from harmful ways and free us from stupid things that cause us distress and shame. Truly they are 10 steps to the good life. Because of God's love, these Commandments are protective in their intent. Through obedience to them by faith and by Gospel power, we are protected from self-destruction and preserved from inflicting unnecessary harm on others.

The Ten Commandments are a blueprint or map for us to guide our thoughts as we make our daily decisions and choices. They are meant to be safety fields to protect us from the devil's assaults against us. Being obedient will give honor and praise to God.

The first three Commandments show our relationship to God. When we look beyond the negatives, God is teaching believers that He loves so much that He gives Himself to us. We are to fear, love and trust God more than any earthly thing. He alone can give us spiritual health and wholeness.

The other seven Commandments show that God loves so much that He wants His creatures to experience love between themselves. Life is sacred, and God wants it preserved and protected. He makes ownership a privilege and responsibility and so entrusts us with possessions and property.

As God brought His people out of bondage in Egypt, so He will deliver us from our sins and slaveries, *"I am the Lord Your God, who brought you out of Egypt, out of the land of slavery"* (Ex. 20:2). It is significant that the Ten Commandments follow this reminder of deliverance from bondage, showing us how to be free from our own sinful nature and its destructive power.

The Ten Commandments are recorded in Exodus 20:3-17. Please read them now before continuing.

God gave the Commandments for three purposes:

1) **A fence, curb or a restraint**: God's Law helps us preserve order in the world by keeping our and others' wicked actions

within limits.  Just as a curb marks the boundaries of a street or road, so God's Law shows us what is out of bounds.

2)  **A mirror**: God's Law works in our minds and hearts to show God's hatred and condemnation for sin.  Just as a mirror shows us what we look like, so the Law shows us the naked truth about ourselves and allows us to see the mistakes of which we are guilty.  We are shown how selfish, proud or deceitful we may be.

3)  **A guide**: God's Law tells us the actions and way of life which are pleasing to God.  It urges us to put our faith into practice.  This is called the third use of the Law - a guide for believers.

*Which function is illustrated in the following passages? Place a ✓ in the appropriate box.*

|  | Curb | Mirror | Guide |
|---|---|---|---|
| Psalm 119:105 |  |  |  |
| Romans 3:20 |  |  |  |
| Romans 7:7 |  |  |  |
| Romans 12:1-2 |  |  |  |
| 1 Tim.1:9-10 |  |  |  |

Pervading all of this is God's great love and His promises which show that He is serious about wanting us to keep all His Commandments, and that He wants to keep us safe in this life and keep us as His own throughout eternity. His Commandments are rooted in His very being.  His loving will for us is to do good in praise to Christ.  The Commandments establish God's place in our lives and the priorities and values we are to adopt.  Can you see how the Commandments function as a curb, mirror and guide?

The Ten Commandments as a goal for godliness provide the foundation upon which Christian character is built.  Godliness is composed of the essential elements of the fear of God, the love of God, and the desire for God.  This is the good life we should seek.  The power for godly character comes from God, but the responsibility for decisions in developing and displaying that character is ours.

*How are the Ten Commandments a blessing and grace event?*


Go to God in prayer and thank Him for the Ten Commandments as a blessing and guide to you, and ask Him to overcome any weaknesses discovered as you consider them as a mirror or curb. After your time of prayer, spend a minute in silence. Record any thoughts you might have below.


## Day Two -- Three Commandments for a Healthy Relationship with God

The First Commandment is, "*YOU SHALL NOT MAKE FOR YOURSELF AN IDOL IN THE FORM OF ANYTHING IN HEAVEN ABOVE OR ON THE EARTH BENEATH OR IN THE WATERS BELOW. YOU SHALL NOT BOW DOWN TO THEM OR WORSHIP THEM*" (Ex. 20:4-5).

1.  *What problem is exposed in these verses?*




2.  *What are some of the main idolatries in our culture which need attention?*


**Week Ten**                                                    198

Egypt gave the Israelites many idols and gods who were worshipped with the thought they would get the maximum number of blessings. The true God was not just another god to be added to the list, but the only God who was to be worshipped.

We give glory to God above all things by placing His Word and commands above that of anything else, by considering Him as more dear to us than anyone or anything else, and by relying on Him for help more than on anything else. Our main goal is to glorify God as we fear and revere Him, love Him, and trust Him.

Our life-principle is that God is sovereign. Do you know what this word means? God possesses supreme power. He does not allow divided loyalty. Jesus gave a New Testament version of the First Commandment in Matthew 4:10: "Worship the Lord your God, and serve Him only" (i.e., give adoration to the one True God, not many gods).

False gods give promise of big hopes which they cannot deliver. False gods manipulate people by offering counterfeits of what the divine, eternal God has to offer. There is no support available from a false god. The true God is a divine Person in heaven, while earthly gods have mouths, eyes and ears, but they cannot speak, see or hear (Ps. 115:3-8). Letting God hold the central place in our lives keeps money, a good life, and work from turning into gods for us.

The Second Commandment is, *"YOU SHALL NOT MISUSE THE NAME OF THE LORD YOUR GOD, FOR THE LORD WILL NOT HOLD ANYONE GUILTLESS WHO MISUSES HIS NAME"*(Ex. 20:7).

God's name is every expression which He uses to refer to Himself. God's name displays what He has to offer in His relationship with us. Our use of His name affects our relations with Him.

**Week Ten**  199

When we are adopted into God's family, we are identified with His name.  He is Father of the family of which we are members by faith in Jesus.  Our language and the use of His name declare our reverence of Him, and the value we place upon our relationship with Him.  The way we use His name shows how we feel about Him.

Abuse of a name, whether of spouse, children, friends or God, is demeaning.  The way we treat God's or other's names indicates our attitude toward Him and others.  Thus, thoughtless or cursing references to Jesus Christ or God almighty are as degrading as angrily cursing in His name.

As we use God's name with the respect it deserves, we will use it to pray, to give thanks, to praise Him and to honor Him.  He loves us so much that He has given us His name, for we are known as His people.  Valuing that privilege, we will not profane our spiritual family's Father.  We dare not be casual in matters that are a matter of faith in God.

1.  *As a Christian you may not be guilty of using God's name as profanity. How then does this Commandment apply to you?*

2.  *How do we harm our own names when we use God's name in vain?*

The Third Commandment is, *"REMEMBER THE SABBATH DAY BY KEEPING IT HOLY.  Six days you shall labor and do all your work, but the seventh day is a Sabbath to your Lord your God. On it, you shall not do any work . . . "* (Ex. 20:8-10).

In the Old Testament God set aside the seventh day (Saturday) as a required day of rest and worship, dedicated to the Lord. Sabbath means rest. The Sabbath was a sign pointing to Jesus, who is our rest. Since Jesus has come as our Savior and Lord, God no longer requires us to observe the Sabbath day and other holy days of the Old Testament. God does require Christians to worship together, but He has not specified any particular day. Churches typically worship together on Sundays because that is the day Christ rose from the dead. Worship on other days is no less valid (Rom. 14:5-6). We are to set aside a time to honor God through worship and rest to refresh our spirits.

This commandment is about worshipful communication with our Creator-Redeemer-Sanctifier. Regular contact with God keeps our relationship strong with Him, avoiding all disruptions.

1. *Many people equate the keeping of this Commandment as "going to church." How is the real intent of this Commandment different than "spending an hour in worship"?*

2. *What does Sabbath mean, and how do we benefit from it? One a scale of 1-10 with 10 the highest, how would you rate your own life of worship? How could it be better?*

Christians have two tasks or works: glorifying God through our occupations, and by worship. The intention of this

Commandment is that we gain an intimacy with God through Bible study, worship, and relaxation. Our regular times of worship and study during the week individually and together as a congregation melds and weaves our beings into greater unity with the Divine Being.

In worship we show God's worth and remember the mighty things He has done in forgiving our sins and rescuing us from slavery. We worship God through Creator-awareness and creature-attention because He is worthy as one who saved us.

Stress and tension which block communication must be relieved by rest. Times of quiet, rest, relaxation and worship are obviously the solution to relieve the pressure of the modern jungle of cars, buses, commerce, concrete and technology. Life, like traveling, makes us tired. Our journey through life is filled with events that sap our energy and strength. Mental and Spiritual exhaustion can creep up on us gradually in life, as well as travel, and the cure requires more than just a nap or an hour away from it all. God shows that we are to have a day of rest, that is how we should plan our Sundays.

During a time of worship or Bible study, we can retreat from the world and relax in an atmosphere conducive to communication with the One who knows and loves us with an undying love. Thus, we communicate and build a closer relationship with Him. Here our emotional batteries are recharged, attitudes realigned and our faith strengthened.

God must be worshipped in spirit and in truth, and He should be reverenced in all our deeds and words. Our bodies need rest and our spirits need constant regular refreshing through Bible study and worship. Pray about this. After a moment of silence, record any thoughts you might have below.

**Week Ten**

## Day Three and Four -- Seven Commandments for Loving Relationships and Keeping Life Sacred

The Fourth Commandment is, *"HONOR YOUR FATHER AND MOTHER, SO THAT YOU MAY LIVE LONG ON THE LAND THE LORD YOUR GOD IS GIVING YOU"* (Ex. 20:12).

This commandment establishes parents as God's representatives and shows the order of proper family life. It reveals that children are to respect, love, obey and serve parents and their authority. They are not to despise parents by speaking or acting disrespectfully, by rebelling against them, or by causing them sorrow. It also applies to other authority figures in our lives that are God's representatives. This includes those in government, at school, at work and in the church.

God has given a special rank or distinction to fathers and mothers, higher than all other human positions except those in civil authority.

*What do these verses say about behavior toward parents?*

| | |
|---|---|
| Deut. 20:18-21 | |
| Eph. 6:2-3 | |
| 2 Tim. 3:1-2 | |

God has given parents many guidelines for raising their children. God's desire is that families are a place where each person's honor is protected and treasured. Unfortunately, we live in an age in which some parents are disobedient to God and teach their children badly, even sometimes giving them physical, emotional, verbal and spiritual abuse. Such children can become emotional cripples and spiritual orphans. Those who have

**Week Ten**

experienced it, should not transfer their alienation to God. They should avoid self-pity. They should know that God is a faithful Father who gives us what our earthly parents do not give. If we cannot depend on parents, we can always depend on God.

*1. How does parents' disobedience to God cause a "cycle of sin," beginning with the children, going from generation to generation?*



*2. When may we have to refuse to obey those in authority?*



The Fifth Commandment is, *"YOU SHALL NOT MURDER"*(Ex. 20:13).

Human life is so sacred to God that He commands protection of everyone's body and life as His gift to every human being. It is a terrible crime to shorten or take away life from anyone: "...and from each man, too, I will demand an accounting for the life of his fellow man. Whoever sheds the blood of man, by man shall his blood be shed; for in the image of God has God made man"(Gen. 9:5-6).

*What we see today in society is a devaluing of life on every front. What are some of the symptoms you have observed that indicates society is ignoring God's law regarding murder?*



Life is so important that only God or His appointed representatives in government have the right to end a person's life

(Deut. 32:39; Ps. 31:15; Rom. 13:4). An individual's life-span is valuable because once a person dies, that is the end, leading to judgment.

Accidental killing, justifiable homicide, killing in a just war and capital punishment were not considered murder in the Old Testament (Num. 35:23; Ex. 21:12ff; 22:2). Murder is violating a person's existence and his relationship with God, for God has invested His creative self in the design of our bodies which are fearfully and wonderfully made (Ps. 113:14).

We are to protect life as a precious gift of God. The human body is a precious resource for productivity and enjoyment in life. God, the Giver of life and health, wants us to avoid doing whatever needlessly destroys, harms, shortens or endangers life and health. This means that we should promote quality and length of life through good nutrition, exercise and adequate sleep.

What about the unborn? Are they pre-human, just a fetus which has no value until born? There is no distinction made in the Scriptures between babies in the womb and those already born, as Elizabeth's baby before birth was given a name (Luke 1:41-44) and identified equally after birth (Luke 18:15).

*What do the following verses say about God's view of the unborn?*

| | |
|---|---|
| **Ex. 21:22-23** | |
| **Ps. 139:13-16** | |
| **Jer. 1:5** | |

God creates each person to know and resemble Himself as a child does a father. Because of this, no one has a right to kill a baby in its prenatal home any more than one does to kill an adult in the family home. God designed the womb to be the safest refuge as a home is for a person, yet abortionists have made it the most dangerous place for a human being to be.

We know too much about the unique features and identity of the unborn child to make the mistake of improperly calling a baby a "part" of the mother's body as though it is a disposable organ.  The unborn child developing within the mother's body is clearly a separate human being entitled to care and protection by the mother and all society.

God gave life enormous worth.  We are to respect it and hold on to it and to protect the lives of others also.

1.  *What is our responsibility in protecting our own life as it relates to this Commandment?*

2.  *How should we help others protect their lives?  How does this relate to driving, abortion, mercy killing?*

3.  *How does a world view that embraces evolution make it easier for us to devalue human life?*

The Sixth Commandment is, *"YOU SHALL NOT COMMIT ADULTERY"* (Ex. 20:14).

The purpose of the commandment is to keep God's gift of sex pure in our bodies and to keep marriage holy.  It is designed to protect the health of the body and the sanctity of family life.

**Week Ten**                                      206

Adultery is the breaking of a relationship with God in another person because it violates God's will and another person. It leaves emotional scars and physical diseases that afflict the guilty and innocent alike. The sex urge is one of the strongest instincts which in itself is not wrong, for God has given it to us. Because of sin, sex easily gets out of control so that a something good becomes an evil, harmful thing.

Jesus emphasized this commandment by applying purity even to the heart, equating even the sexual look outside of marriage as an act of adultery (Matt. 5:28). In 1 Corinthians 7, Paul clearly shows us that marriage is to be a life-long one man-one woman relationship and that sexual faithfulness is a part of that arrangement. Sex needs marriage, and marriage needs sex. Sexual sins assault Christ's Lordship in one's life, for Christ will not be united with a fornicator (1 Cor. 6:19).

God also condemns homosexuality as sin (1 Cor. 6:9-10; Rom. 1:26-27). The homosexual lifestyle is not an alternate one that is acceptable to God. Sinful sex is never an option.

*Why did God command marriage?*

*How is sexuality in marriage expressed in terms of God's design?*

| | |
|---|---|
| *Fulfilling the sexual role in marriage 1 Cor. 7:3* | |
| *Insuring sexual fulfillment 1 Cor.s 7:4-5* | |

| The use of pornography *Matt. 5:28* | |
| --- | --- |

*How does expressing God's design for sex in marriage help us avoid sexual sin?*

**For singles:**

*How are you to deal with sex in accordance with God's plan for your life?  Do you struggle with this issue?*

The Seventh Commandment is, *"YOU SHALL NOT STEAL"*(Ex. 20:15).

Personal property is a sacred trust from God. This commandment addresses the proper attitude toward God's property placed into our care.  The positive side of this commandment stresses the commitment to unselfish work, the importance of earning, the obligations that go with owning, and the sacred stewardship of managing possessions and property.

God gives to whom He pleases, giving more to some and less to others.  All are to be faithful caretakers of what has been entrusted to them (Prov. 22:2; 1 Cor. 4:2).

***Read the following verses to see what God's Word says about our work and possessions .***

| *Ps. 145:15-16* | |
| --- | --- |

| *Eccl. 5:18* | |
|---|---|
| *Luke 12:25* | |
| *1 Cor. 16:2* | |
| *Eph. 4:28* | |
| *Eph. 5:20* | |
| *1 Tim. 5:8* | |

A growing problem in our society today is gambling. It is driven by our desire to get something for nothing. It is really stealing. Gambling, which takes from one to give to another, really has no winners, only losers. Even most winners are losers: "...Nor to put their hope in wealth, which is so uncertain, but to put their hope in God..."(1 Tim. 6:17). People who want to get money from gambling and lotteries instead of work should recognize that this can lead to ruin and destruction: "People who want to get rich fall into temptation and a trap..."(1 Tim. 6:9). Gambling money is won at someone else's expense. It exploits human weakness that makes people's desperate situations even more critical with the financial loss of what they bet.

1.  *How could you steal from your employer?  How would a Christian be tempted to think that way?*

*2.  God owns everything.  We are managers for Him.  Is it possible to steal from God?  How?*




The Eighth Commandment is, *"YOU SHALL NOT GIVE FALSE TESTIMONY AGAINST YOUR NEIGHBOR"*(Ex. 20:16).

This means speaking and listening to the truth about others, and refusing to listen to slander, gossip or character assassination.  A good name is important because it determines whether or not other people will respect and trust us.

*What do the following passages say about the way we should speak of others?*

| | |
|---|---|
| Prov. 11:13 | |
| Prov. 19:5 | |
| James 4:11 | |

God wants us to defend the good name of others, speak well of them and interpret words and actions in the kindest possible way.  The tongue has power to communicate both good and evil (James 3:5-10).

Precautions to help prevent us from bearing false witness include the evaluating of the source of information, resisting exaggeration, and avoiding half-truths.  Let every Christian accept the principle, "If there are any criticisms, talk **to** people, not **about** people."  We should be governed by telling truth about each other in love (Eph. 4:15).

*1.  How should we act when conversation concerns others' reputations?*


**Week Ten**                                      210

*2. How do we harm ourselves when we gossip about others?*


*3. How do we show love by how we speak about one another?*


The Ninth and Tenth Commandments are, *"YOU SHALL NOT COVET YOUR NEIGHBOR'S HOUSE. YOU SHALL NOT COVET YOUR NEIGHBOR'S WIFE, OR HIS MANSERVANT OR MAIDSERVANT, HIS OX OR DONKEY, OR ANYTHING THAT BELONGS TO YOUR NEIGHBOR"*(Ex. 20:17).

Coveting is the sinful desire for anything, wanting something which we have no right to have or seeking to get it in a sinful way. Sinful desire leads to coveting: *"After desire has conceived, it gives birth to sin, and sin, when it is full-grown, gives birth to death" (James 1:16).* Covetousness is desire that has become uncontrolled, wild, or gone wrong. It drives people to steal and leads some to lawsuits in an attempt to get something away from another person.

Covetousness takes us back to the First Commandment, because it puts a false god in the place of the true God in our lives. Greed seeks first the kingdom of things, not the kingdom of God.

We ought to desire only that which is within the will of God. We should help our neighbor keep his property and be happy when he owns something we do not have.

*1. What are dishonest practices in business that result from coveting?*


**Week Ten**                                               211

2.    *Why is it dangerous to want more and more money and possessions according to 1 Timothy 6:6-17?*


## Day Five -- Summary and Conclusion of the Commandments

God says of all these commandments, *"I, the Lord your God, am a jealous God, punishing the children for the sins of the fathers to the third and fourth generation of those who hate Me, but showing love to a thousand generations of those who love Me and keep My commandments"*(Ex. 20:5-6).

God calls any breaking of His commandments sin (missing the mark), transgression (crossing the forbidden line), and iniquity (failing to measure up perfectly). God threatens to punish on earth and in eternity all those who disobey His commandments. This threat tells us that God is jealous and serious about wanting us to be His obedient children and keep everyone of His commandments. Disobedience is so serious that children and following generations may suffer for this. God has warned us of this penalty so that we will take His Law seriously. The punishment for sin is God's anger, death now, and separation from God forever.

*How have you seen people bring blessing or punishment on themselves by their attitude toward God's Laws?*


God promises grace and every blessing to those who love Him and keep His commandments. His gracious promise should lead us to love and trust Him and gladly obey what He requests.

Under grace we look to these commands as freedom from slavery and protection from harm. He assures blessings to those who keep His commandments (Luke 10:25-28). Jesus promises, "Do this, and you will live."

There is no hope for us in the Law. By nature we are condemned by God's Law because we have sinned, cannot keep the commandments, and deserve nothing but punishment. We can only turn to God for mercy, telling Him that we are sorry for our sins and asking Him to forgive us.

Our only hope is in Christ. For Jesus' sake, God is gracious to us and blesses us. Jesus kept the commandments for us and paid the penalty for our sins. Through faith in Jesus we are God's children. Because of this, we love and trust God, and gladly do His will. The commandments show us how we can please our loving Father.

A lawyer asked the question, "Teacher, which commandment is the greatest in Moses' teachings?" Jesus answered him, "Love the Lord your God with all your heart and with all your soul and with all your might. This is the first and greatest commandment. And the second is like it. Love your neighbor as yourself. All the Law and the Prophets hang on these two commandments"(Matt. 22:36-40). The terms heart, soul and mind are used to stress that we are to love God with our total being:

1) With all our **heart**, all our powers of the will, informed by God's Word so that we might know what we should and should not do;

2) With all our **soul**, all our powers of emotion, developing Christ-like qualities in service to God and others;

3) With all our **mind** or powers of intellect, being equipped through knowledge and understanding to be edifiers of our fellow men.

The great commandment involves two parts:

1)  Loving God with our whole being;

2)  Loving our neighbors as ourselves.

This is the sum total of all the commandments, which are eternal truths revealed by God for Christian living to those He created and redeemed.  They establish God's place in our lives, and how we are to value other human beings.  God gave us the Law because He cares about us and desires the best for us.

*1.  We see care in Jesus' actions. Read Luke 19:41-46.  Why was Jesus weeping?*

*2.  How does this account show God's anger over sin and His love for sinful people?*

*3.  Complete the following sentence: I am thankful for the Ten Commandments because . . .*

## Take the High Road, not the Low Road

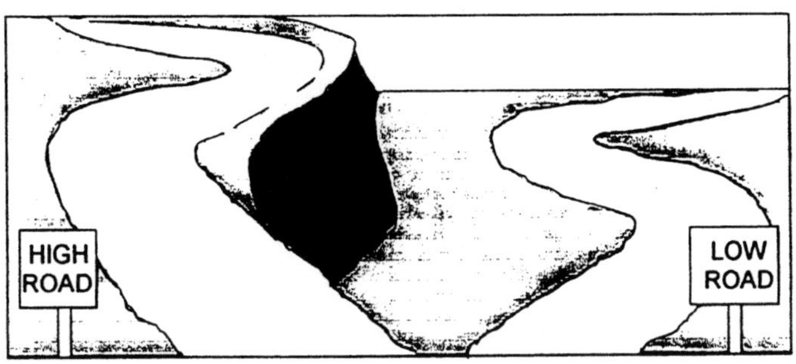



Taking the high road means that by God's grace we have committed ourselves to keep our minds on the Ten Commandments at all times so that when we face a temptation, we will not ask, "Will I or will I not do this?," but say, "In my baptism, I have been committed and empowered to live the Christian life. God, my Father, gives me strength not to avoid this sin, but instead to glorify Jesus." That attitude will cause us to do what is right even when no one is looking, but God. Right now is the right time to speak to God about this and to make a life-long commitment of taking the high road of the Ten Commandments in preparation for all the dangerous intersections or curves which you will travel in your journey of life. **Please record your thoughts in making this commitment to travel on the high road.**

At this time, you have accepted the boundaries of the high road which God has set for you. Freedom to do anything you want is not an inalienable right in relation to God.  Lifestyle restrictions are not an infringement on the sacred territory.  The Ten Commandments set for us what is "out of bounds" – what is harmful and what devalues our lives.

"There is a way that seems right to a man, but in the end it leads to death"(Prov. 14:12).  That is what is at stake when we face the decision of taking the high road or the low road.  As Christians, we affirm, "Oh how I love Your law!  I meditate on it all day long ... Your Word is a lamp to my feet and a light for my path ...My heart is set on keeping Your decrees to the very end"(Ps. 119:97,105,112).  The world curses these boundaries. Thank God for these boundaries, which free us from slavings.

**Live by Grace, not by the Rules of Pharisees**

The Ten Commandments have been presented as a grace event, as God's will recorded in the Ten Commandments to protect us from harm and destruction.  Human nature wants to make these rules to keep in order to give us credit for our salvation.  The Ten Commandments as God's Law and God's love in the Gospel can be perverted by using them contrary to their purpose, and even substituting human rules as the Pharisees did.

Jesus ran head-on into what someone called the world champion nit-pickers - the Pharisees.  Although the Law of Moses allowed an afternoon snack which Jesus did in taking some grain to eat, the Pharisees became very upset as they accused Jesus of violating the Sabbath rest.  They gave fanatic attention to external details, which Jesus rejected by saying, "The Sabbath was made for man, not man for the Sabbath.  So the Son of Man is Lord even of the Sabbath"(Matt. 2:27-28). This did not allow them to use the Sabbath as a test to make little rules they could keep to protect their religiosity and prove their spirituality.  This was **legalism**.

*Week Ten*                                             216

*Have you ever experienced legalism in a religious setting?  If so, how did you react?*

The Pharisees shared many of Jesus' beliefs, taking seriously Biblical doctrine.  However, their interpretation was faulty in practice, building on a set of traditions which became as holy as God's Law itself.  Jesus harshly criticized them for honoring human traditions over God's Law.

*What are some human traditions that we might be guilty of honoring over God's Law?*

Are you possibly guilty of imposing your requirements on someone else in some way?  Ask yourself:

- *What standards of righteousness do I expect from people? Are they  Biblical? How do I behave when these standards are not met?*

- *What "requirements" do I claim are essential for worship? Are they Biblical or traditional?*

- *What programs or methods do I hold to be essential for our church? Are they Biblical or traditional?*

While the Pharisees understood holiness in terms of rituals and ceremonial actions and separation from sinners, Jesus showed holiness through His image of God involved with human beings as Reconciler, and His radical difference from the world through a life of love.

The legalist, like the Pharisee, is dangerous because he carefully builds his own pattern of living and tries to make it a rule for all Christians, making others prisoners of his expectations. He insists on being both the judge and the jury for the rest of the Christian community. Legalism creates man-made fences which restrict others from living with consciences free from human bondage. The rules of legalism are cultural and personal in their origin, rather than Biblical.

Legalism is a man-made religion which negates the vitality and strength which God's grace brings to life. Such a "rules-religion" will fence us out from the spontaneity of the Gospel, which gives us freedom and maturity. It leads to pride in one's obedience to a set of rules. We must recognize the inadequacy of rules and self-effort which are elevated to divine imperatives.

*What was the Pharisee's problem?  How did Phariseeism and legalism misuse the law?*

**Major Points to Review**

1. *Tell how the Ten Commandments are a blessing for the Christian.*

**Week Ten**                                     218

2. *As you consider the first three Commandments about a healthy relationship with the true God, do you sense any "gods" that may be protecting you from vital worship?*

3. *Regarding the remaining seven Commandments concerning our actions towards others, which of these may be the greatest problem for you?*

4. *Do you find it difficult to make a distinction between your personal requirements (expectations) and God's specific requirements for others? How?*

**OBSERVATIONS/REFLECTIONS ON WHAT YOU STUDIED THIS WEEK:**

1. What matters or issues would you like to know more about? What, if anything, troubled you about what you studied?

2. What new knowledge or insights have you learned?

**Week Ten**                                             219

3. How has your faith grown or been modified?



4. How will this affect your life?

# WEEK ELEVEN

# MY SPIRITUAL FAMILY

Most of us do not enjoy traveling alone. We would rather travel with family or friends with whom we can share our experiences. Others provide vital assistance and enjoyment throughout our journey of life.

Our spiritual rebirth and baptism made Jesus the best companion we can have. He is constantly at our side and is able to sustain us in every situation. We are also spiritual brothers and sisters with all those who confess Jesus as Savior and Lord and who name God as their Father.

All those everywhere who believe in Jesus as Savior are part of the body of Christ or the holy Christian Church. The Holy Spirit calls, gathers, enlightens, sanctifies, and keeps all believers in the Christian Church by the Gospel. The Church is a spiritual family with God as Father. It is found only where the Gospel is proclaimed. This spiritual family of faith is not visible and is called the Invisible Church. When Christians gather together in a congregation, that is the visible church.

The Invisible Church denotes all true believers in Jesus Christ, while the visible church or congregation may contain believers and hypocrites as its members. The Church seems to be a paradox: it is divine/spiritual, a body in which the Spirit of God lives and acts; yet it is human, made up of people who are faulty. It is holy, yet it is composed of sinful people. It experiences the same kind of dichotomy as the Christian, who is both sinner and saint, old self and new self.

*Please define the visible church and the invisible church, and why it is important to know the difference.*

### Day One -- The Body of Christ

God has called Christians into a living, loving community, which is Christ's body, whose head is Christ Himself. Bonding together into Christ's body is an entrance into the reality of God, which is a safe haven from the evil around us.

Jesus is the Head and Lord of the body, as the Holy Spirit is its life and power. Christ's body is spiritual in human form, heavenly in earthly structures, and perfect in imperfect embodiment. It is an organism, not an institution. It exists to fulfill the purposes of God in Christ through regenerated persons on earth for the good of us sinful human beings.

The reality of the body of Christ is key to understanding not only the believer's relationship to God through Jesus Christ, but also his relationship to every other believer in the world. The body of Christ refers to the universal church - all true believers known only by God.

*"... Though all His parts are many, they form one body. So it is with Christ. For we were all baptized by one Spirit into one body -- whether Jews or Greeks, slave or free ... Now the body is not made up of one part but of many" (1 Cor. 12:12-14).*

1. *Reflecting on the above Bible passage and on 1 Cor. 12:27, what role do you seek for your part in God's body according to His call?*

2. *Why do you think many Christian congregations are not actively functioning as a body of Christ in their actions, but only for going to church? What should be done about it?*

Christ makes the whole body fit together and unites it through the support of each member.  As Christians we each have a support role to play in the body.  Your small group is a great place to begin your life of ministry.  Active participation in a small group will give you many opportunities to minister to members and to reach out to people who don't have a relationship with Christ.

*"Instead, speaking the truth in love, we will in all things grow up into Him who is the Head, that is, Christ.  From Him the whole body, joined and held together by every supporting ligament, grows and builds itself up in love, as each part does its work" (Eph. 4:15-16).*

*What is the function of every member according to this passage?*

God's plan for a functioning, growing, witnessing, love-manifesting, serving and powerful church is that every member be a vital organ in the body of Christ.  Each is to be actively involved in the God-given functions so that the whole body can be healthy and nurtured for witness and service.  God's plan for His church gives each of us an opportunity to fulfill God's plan for

**Week Eleven**                                                      **223**

us. As we come to fully realize God's plan for us within His church, we find true fulfillment in all that we do.

Life in the body and spiritual gifts are revealed in Eph. 4:7, 12-16, 1 Cor. 12 and Rom. 12. Read these verses now.

By comparing the church and the human body, Paul developed his analogy along the four themes shown below.

| | |
|---|---|
| Unity - 1 Corinthians 12:12-13 | All believers share the common life in God, where there are no degrees of importance or significance. |
| Diversity - Ephesians 4:7; 1 Corinthians 12:14 | Each believer is uniquely gifted to be very essential to the functioning of the body of Christ. |
| Sovereignty - 1 Corinthians 12:18, 24, 28 | Each believer is exactly what God wants each to be by grace, even though they have choices in their place and role. |
| Harmony - Hebrews 10:25; 1 Peter 3:8; 1 Corinthians 3:4-5 | There is to be no rugged individualism or self-sufficiency that appeals to human selfishness or reason. Rivalry is not acceptable in the body of Christ |

1. *What are some of the spiritual gifts listed in these chapters?*


2. *How do you think you might find out about your spiritual gifts?*


**Week Eleven**                                        **224**

The above Scriptures show us how believers are equipped and held together for God's service. The focus is on members of Christ's body, identifying their abilities which God has given them. We have not chosen the gifts we have, but this was decided by the Ascended Lord. "To each one of us grace has been given as Christ apportioned it"(Eph. 4:7). Our responsibility individually is to discover what gifts Christ has given us as members of His body. One of the best ways to find your spiritual gifts is to follow these simple steps:

1. Ask God in prayer to show you your gifts. Read and reread the passages listed above.
2. Experiment. Try performing various acts of service. Ask for feedback. Examine how you feel, but don't let the voice of fear drown out affirmation you might get from other people.
3. Watch for things to happen. Are people responding to the ministry you are doing?

Jesus promised that He would build His Church which would last forever. Not even the devil will be able to destroy it. This Church is made up of people chosen from all nations and all time. These believers are part of our larger Spiritual family. Jesus Himself is the founder, and all who believe in Him as their Lord are "living stones, built on this foundation." The Holy Spirit, the master builder, builds God's Church through the Word and Sacraments.

*1. How well does the body of Christ work at our church?*

*2. How can we improve "Body life" in our church?*

*3. How is God calling you to participate in improving the "Body life"?*

Go to God in prayer and thank Him that He has given a spiritual gift to all Christians, including you, and ask Him to use you in a way in which He desires. After your time of prayer, spend a minute in silence. Record any thoughts you might have below.

## Day Two -- Building Christian Community

Unity and community are vital qualities of the body of Christ, the Church. Despite the greatest possible variety of people - of every ethnic background, nation, personality, economic level, age, etc. - brought into one community of Christian beliefs by God through baptism, all are molded into one community to function together. In the same world where dysfunctional groups and families live, our Christian family is united with our individual dissimilarities into one family in Jesus. God builds us into a Christian community.

No person is complete by oneself, and no one has been entrusted with everything. Completeness is found only in mutual caring and sharing through Christian community. All Christians need the body environment if they are to be truly strong, where each can be helped. An ideal place to experience this environment is in your small group.

*The need for us to live in community is filled in a positive way through our church, our small groups and our families. Can*

**Week Eleven**

*you think of examples of counterfeit community that people rely on when God's plan for community has been ignored or shattered by sin?*

The words **fellowship** and **community** are sometimes used loosely to mean times when groups of church people merely get together for some event. Those activities can be found shallow and meaningless when evaluated from the divine perspective rather than the earthly. People can be very isolated and fragmented, even though they are getting together in churchly tasks. Christian community is built when individuals grow together to be more obedient followers of Christ as a result of hearing the Word. In community, we hear the Word from others who are close to us and know our needs. This makes God's Word very personal.

*In what settings do members of our church hear the Word? Who is proclaiming it in each setting? What are the benefits of each setting?*

Christian community is not built on what people want to hear or only good news. One of the proofs of genuine community is the ability to listen to bad news about oneself and others, accepting the Law and God's judgment and then gaining relief through the good news of forgiveness of all our sins. True community does not allow shallow spirituality or scapegoating, but insists on loving confrontation by the Law and Gospel.

**Week Eleven**                                                    227

The mutual responsibility and interdependence of individual members of the body is best seen and understood in a survey of the "one another" messages of the epistles.

"Love one another, even as I have loved you"(John 13:34).

"Each member belongs to all the others"(Rom. 12:5).

"Be devoted to one another in brotherly love"(12:10a).

"Honor one another above yourselves"(12:10c).

"Live in harmony with one another"(12:16a).

"Accept one another, then, just as Christ accepted you"(15:7).

"Have equal concern for each other"(1 Cor. 12:25).

"Serve one another"(Gal. 5:13).

"Carry each other's burdens"(6:2).

"Submit to one another"(5:21).

"Teach and admonish one another"(3:16).

"Encourage one another and build each other up"(1 Thes. 5:11).

"Confess your sins to each other and pray for each other"(James 5:16).

We can see that each member is to function and contribute to the process of edifying or building up each other. This is for every believer, not just enthusiasts. We are not given the choice of whether or not we want to function this way. God made us dependent upon each other.

A church must be a safe place to express pain and hurt. It must offer people help and support for their heartaches and abuse. No wrongs should be ignored, but all problems should be addressed through repentance and forgiveness. None of this can be accomplished by human effort, but only by the Holy Spirit by the Gospel of reconciliation.

Your small group is an ideal setting for "one another" ministry to take place. It takes much work to achieve the safety of a healthy Christian community, but the results are worth the effort. Openness to each other requires that we be vulnerable, having the willingness even to be wounded, to cry with those who cry and to hurt with those who hurt. We do not give the impression that we are without weaknesses, for we are not. Only the wounded can really help heal. People in crisis should feel free to come to and participate in the Christian community. No Christian community can ever be 100% healthy, having no spiritually sick members. "Are we on target? How are we doing?" are questions that will be regularly asked in a healthy community.

*How would you rate community/ relationship building in our church? How could community be improved? What is the biggest barrier to improving community?*

To allow false expectations can hurt or destroy a community. Only Biblical standards are to be taught and allowed, while all human assumptions and viewpoints which deny truth are to be prohibited. It is urgent to be aware of the perceptions that people bring to community, especially ones who carry traditional prejudices that fit rigid organizations more than a loving Christian community.

*Have you seen Christian community suffer because of human views that are not supported by Scripture? How?*

*The following passages reveal God's requirements for community within the church.*

| 1 Cor. 1:10 | |
|---|---|

**Week Eleven**

| 2 Cor. 13:11 | |
|---|---|
| Eph. 4:3, 13 | |

*Why do these Scriptures not allow diversity in doctrine for congregational fellowship?*

*What fellowship disruption is discussed in the following passages?*

| 1 Tim. 6:3-5 | |
|---|---|
| Titus 1:11 | |
| 2 Peter 2:1-2 | |

*What are we to do when individuals destroy fellowship by false doctrine or sinful acts?*

The Christian community is strengthened when its individuals die to themselves as Jesus suggests. Strength is gained only when we recognize our brokenness. This requires emptying of ourselves, our carnal wills.

A characteristic of the community is that it communicates. Each member has mutual access to each other

**Week Eleven** 230

without restrictions.  The standards of good communication offer the basic principles of community-building.  There will be open doors to each other and no locks on those doors, or no doors slammed in faces.

The 21st Century Church should seek to learn the basics of the 1st Century Church to make certain that its essential nature is restored where it may have been disfigured.  A little "Jesus" veneer on the institutional church is not Biblical and does not enrich the lives of people.  Spiritual formation happens most compellingly and completely in the context of Christian community.  One of the best places to experience this is in a small group.  When we open our hearts to God, we must also open our hearts to other believers.

Go to God in prayer and ask Him to help you and all members of your congregation to be functioning members of the Body to make yours a healthy church.  After your time of prayer, spend a minute of silence.  Record any thoughts  you might have below.


## Day Three -- Members of Christ's Kingdom

By faith, you are a citizen in God's kingdom.  God governs through Jesus Christ as King of the entire universe.  God is the Sovereign Ruler, who guides the stars in their courses and controls the laws of nature.  He directs the destinies of nations and the life of every individual.  Our lives are under His rule and guidance, and He defends us for our good.

Christ is King, who with His almighty power rules, governs and protects His church, and finally leads it to glory. Jesus left us with these words before He ascended into heaven, *"And surely I am with you always, to the very end of the earth"*(Matt. 28:18-20).

Christ's kingdom is not of this world (John 18:36), for this world is evil. He enters the world to rule for good. His is the kingdom of grace, the church on earth. As citizens of Jesus' kingdom, He rules us with love and grace. He reigns in order to prepare us for the kingdom of heaven and glory. When we pray, "Your kingdom come," as Jesus taught us, we are asking that His kingdom might be evident in our lives and seen in our conduct as His citizens. Much of the past ten weeks has been spent establishing the basis for our citizenship (Christ) and examining our behavior and conduct to see if they are reflective our citizenship.

God's purpose for His church on earth is to share the Gospel in an evil world. We pray that He would extend His kingdom of grace on earth through the Gospel in reaching the lost. Christ's kingdom on earth exists for this purpose. The church and the resulting Christian community are instruments God uses to carry out His attack on the evil of the world. It can be a tough battle because we must face the evil in our lives and the evil in the world.

Our comfort is that Jesus, our Friend, is the powerful Ruler of all things, watching with tender care over us. God set Him at His right hand in heaven. At His name, every knee should bow and confess that Jesus is Lord.

At the same time, the devil has set up his kingdom of darkness in opposition to God's kingdom to make it look like beautiful light. The two kingdoms are in constant conflict. As Christians, we are at the center of this battle. Satan uses attractive but deadly methods to lure people away from God. Our steady "Spiritual Warfare" reveals the evil power which we face from the kingdom of Satan. God gives His sure promise that we are plugging into the right power source when we give our mind

**Week Eleven**                                                    232

to Christ. "We demolish arguments and every pretension that sets itself up against the knowledge of God, and we take captive every thought to make it obedient to Christ"(2 Cor. 10:3-5).

*As a citizen of God's kingdom, you will be asked many times to confront Satan and his schemes in your own life and the life of others. How willing are you to engage in this battle? Why do you feel this way?*

As a member of Christ's Kingdom, God has given us authority over evil forces (Luke 10:18-19). Besides the sin we find in our own lives, we can see how evil is affecting the world. Greed, materialism and the misuse of the gift of sex are outward signs accepted as normal behavior by many. The kingdom of darkness presents psychic phenomena and occult powers appearing to be displayed through a person which is not of God. Many people are deceived. They depend on a daily horoscope, astrology, or even palm reading. Others claim to have the gift of prophecy through dreams and visions. These are part of the kingdom of evil. Our job as citizens is to recognize evil and through God's Holy Spirit fight back.

*How have you been trained for the battle against evil? What will you do to be fully prepared?*

Go to God in prayer and thank Him for the powerful word and name of Jesus in your battle against evil, and ask Him to make you fully alert and ready for any attacks on the devil.

**Week Eleven**

After your time of prayer, spend a minute of silence.  Record any thoughts you might have below.


## Day Four -- My Congregation/Local Church

Because God required believers as His spiritual family to come together to grow and expand, the early Christians carried out the Great Commission by organizing congregations in different areas like Corinth, Ephesus, Galatia, and Thessalonica. Congregations (visible groups) differ from the Holy Christian Church (invisible church).  The visible church includes both believers and non-believers, for we cannot look into other people's hearts.

The basic foundation on which the visible church rests is a clear understanding of the Christian faith and the mission of the church.  The mission of the church was given to us by Jesus before He ascended.  Jesus said, *"All authority in heaven and on earth has been given to me.  Therefore go and make disciples of all nations, baptizing them in the name of the Father and of the Son and of the Holy Spirit, and teaching them to obey everything I have commanded you. And surely I am with you always, to the very end of the age"*(Matt. 28:18-20).

Our mission is clear.  Make disciples by baptizing and teaching obedience to all that God has commanded.  The questions come when begin to try and decide the best way to accomplish this goal.  We know that we must be faithful to God's Word and the Sacraments of Baptism and the Lord's Supper.  The sole objective of the church in its institutional form is the realization of the Biblical purpose.  That mission is basically spiritual, not political, ethical or psychological.  It does not rely on the force of the Law, but on the Gospel of grace and the power of love. The visible church uses organizational forms and functional approaches to communicate the message.

*How do you evaluate our congregation related to obedience to the Great Commission and fulfillment of its Biblical purpose? Are we on target, or have we been distracted from the core focus or true purpose?*


The nature of God, the Christian Gospel, and the body of Christ have already determined the goals and objectives toward which the local church should be moving as it seeks to fulfill its mission. It must be the mouthpiece of God, not of the people. The church is the only institution on earth whose great mission is to help people find God and eternal life through Jesus Christ.

The New Testament does not prescribe earthly forms for functions and tasks of the church. When form is named in the Bible, it is incomplete and partial, varying from one setting to another. Only later through traditions did the institution allow forms to become sacred while functions sometimes became perverted. We need to look behind the facade and traditions to find the real meaning of the church at various times in history. The church should never plan its work as though it is merely an extension of the past or merely renewing its traditions.

*How have you seen tradition defended as a Biblical requirement? If so, what effect has this had on our church?*

Wherever God's people are, there must be a functioning church. Wherever we have function, we need form. We cannot have an organism without organization. We cannot communicate a message without a method. We cannot teach truth without developing some kind of tradition or style. The question is whether a specific form or tradition is presented as an absolute Scriptural requirement.

*What should be expected of members in the congregation? How can we communicate these expectations in a loving way?*

What is the foundation for a healthy, functioning church? There must be these components with Christ as the foundation: an acceptance of truth, an awareness of God's presence, a responsiveness to God's Word, a sensitivity to the reality of sin, a lively and edifying fellowship, fruitfulness in member's lives, and strong evangelistic activity.

When any emphasis in the church interferes in any way with the Biblical task to use the resources of Christ faithfully, and to minister more effectively to the needs of people, then the church has lost its way. The church is not programs and buildings, but people as the body of Christ. Members are not tools for church leaders to use to get the church work done.

The institutionalizing of the church can be seen in the maintenance or survival approach in managing its work and financial resources. This will reduce people to little more than cogs in the machinery. This suppresses God's Word, while man's word controls with human views of the work of the church. Under these conditions, members are reactive and surrender their initiative for their service and ministry. They feel they must be ministered to, rather than be ministering members.

1.   *In what ways can the church lose its way?  What can be
     done about it?*

2.   *How can members become captive or enslaved to one way
     of doing things which may hamper growth and progress?*

The church is a community affair.  You yourself are not
the church.  I am not the church. We (all of God's disciples) are
the church, and we behave as the church by assembling together,
studying together, worshipping, edifying, exhorting, loving,
helping, and giving.  Where there is no assembling for various
functions, there is no church.  The Word of God is the only power
and authority which is capable to govern this church.

Go to God in prayer and thank Him for the ways in which
our congregation is faithful to God, and ask Him to make
whatever changes are necessary.  After your time of prayer, spend
a minute of silence.  Record any thoughts you may have below.

**Day Five -- The Office of the Keys - Caring/
Confronting/ Edifying Relationships**

Christ has given keys to the church related to caring,
confronting and edifying relationships to help us all keep strong in
the faith.  Our life together is permeated by speaking the word of
Law and Gospel to each other to remain healthy members of
Christ's body.  This also means ultimately to speak the word of

**Week Eleven**                                    237

Law to those who are weak and erring.  The latter is called the keys to the kingdom, which Christ gives as a special power and right either to forgive sins (the loosing key) or to refuse to forgive sins (the binding key).

Jesus said, *"I will give you the keys of the kingdom of heaven.  Whatever you bind on earth will be bound in heaven, and whatever you loose on earth will be loosed in heaven"*(Matt.16:19).  *"If you forgive anyone his sins, they are forgiven; if you do not forgive them, they are not forgiven"*(John 20:23).

The use of the keys is that special power and right which Christ gave to His church on earth to forgive the sins of repentant sinners, but to refuse it to those who do not repent. These keys are given only to God's people, the priesthood of all believers, the church.  Christians are called priests in 1Peter 2:9, *"You are a chosen people, a royal priesthood, a holy nation, a people belonging to God, that you may declare the praises of Him who called you out of darkness into His wonderful light."*

The purpose of the keys is to keep people in the faith or to win them back.  God wants us to use the binding key to try to lead impenitent sinners to repent as God's terrible judgment is announced to them.  "Repent...and turn to God so that your sins may be wiped out"(Acts 3:19).  God wants us to use the loosing key to forgive the sins of a penitent sinner: "You are to forgive and comfort him, so that he will not be overwhelmed by excessive sorrow"(2 Cor. 2:7).

The keys are administered publicly through the pastor (1 Peter 5:2), the office of the public ministry.  Only men whom the Holy Spirit has led the congregation to choose, may serve as pastors in the congregation (divine call).  The congregation has the authority from Christ to call a pastor to preach and teach the Word of God publicly, including using the binding and loosing keys through the action of the congregation.

**Week Eleven**                                   238

The key to understanding the pastoral ministry is to see the common mission of the church and how all people in the church work together towards achieving this mission. Though we are all priests participating in this mission, God calls some to the public ministry. In this role, they preach the Word, administer the sacraments and administer the keys for the congregation.

The priesthood of all believers is seen through our support of the pastor working jointly to be obedient to the Great Commission. Our role is to minister to one another through a loving attitude of caring/confronting/edifying. Through our actions, we support the pastor's ministry of the Word.

*How do you feel about your role of caring, confronting and edifying people in the church? How does this role affect the way you look at your own shortcomings?*

Evangelical confrontation plus caring encourages growth. Truth spoken with love, and judgment blended with grace, will show itself through believers who care enough to stay in faithful relationship with each other. Offending people should receive loving, honest treatment, while the strong give a caring/confronting response. This is what the Bible calls edifying or building each other up in faith, and speaking the word of Law and Gospel to each other. As we uphold the oneness that God gives us in Christ, we maintain unity with one another. Thus a strong support system should be in place in the church.

Sometimes conflict arises between two Christians or offense is given by one. Matthew 18 gives us practical guidance for dealing with those who sin against us. Jesus said in Matthew 18:15-17, *"If your brother sins against you, go and tell him his fault, just between the two of you. If he listens to you, you have*

*won your brother over. But if he will not listen, take one or two
others along, so that every matter may be established by the
testimony of two or three witnesses. 'If he refuses to listen to
them, tell it to the church; and if he refuses to listen even to the
church, treat him as you would a pagan or a tax collector."*

Notice the first step: go and show the person his fault.
Too often our approach is to complain to someone else. This
violates God's approach to dealing with sin. We use this process
to minister to those who are in shackles of sin, and present them
with the opportunity of being liberated from the power of sin in
any and all forms, returning in repentance and faith to the rule of
Christ. Such discipline does not bring division and disunity into
the church. When Biblical principles are followed, the opposite is
true - division and disunity will be overcome and avoided. Failure
to follow God's command for church discipline will result in
disunity of the church until the problem is dealt with scripturally.

How sin is confronted is important. *"Speaking the truth
in love, we will in all things grow up into him who is the Head,
that is, Christ"*(Eph. 4:15).

*1. What is the Office of the Keys, and why is this important
   for our congregation?*




*2. Are the members of your congregation aware of their
   responsibility and the necessity to use the Office of the
   Keys? Why or why not?*


**Week Eleven**                                     240

*3. What happens if a congregation fails in its responsibility to care/edify/confront? How has the failure to confront sin affected relationships between Christians?*

Go to God in prayer and ask Him to make you and all members conscious of their responsibility to edify and care for other Christians who may be weak. After your time of prayer, spend a minute in silence. Record any thoughts you might have below.

## OBSERVATIONS/REFLECTIONS ON WHAT YOU STUDIED THIS WEEK:

1. What matters or issues would you like to know more about? What, if anything, troubled you about what you studied?

2. What new knowledge or insights have you learned?

3. How has your faith grown or been modified?

4. How will this affect your life?

*Week Eleven*

# WEEK TWELVE

# MY HUMAN FAMILY

God made the family the basic social institution on earth, providing an example of the way society should be.  The family is based upon marriage and the sacred union which carries and sustains family life.  Parents are to be models which help children grow into maturity.  The basic family unit is a married couple - husband and wife, expanded by children.

However, culture has changed so much during the past several decades that today there are many one-parent families and singles, who have varying degrees of challenges in achieving healthy relationships.  In the midst of it all, God's love and the Gospel of forgiveness are the healing and the feeding process for achieving visible goals which Christians set for themselves.

What influences from your family of origin have contributed to your present understanding and beliefs concerning family life? (Make a √ at the appropriate place for your private use.)

- Christian family with loving and caring parents and siblings, but with normal weaknesses.
- Christian family with regular conflicts which were seldom resolved.
- Non-Christian family with loving relations between parents and children with normal weaknesses.
- Non-Christian family with regular conflicts which were not resolved.
- Combination of two-parent and single-parent families.

- Single-parent family with good relations and normal weaknesses.
- Single-parent family with conflicts.
- Severe abusive treatment.

*How has your experience in your family of origin affected your current attitude and conduct? (For personal use.)*

As you assess your own situation, what are your personal circumstances?  (Make a √ at the appropriate place.)
- Single and generally happy
- Single but waiting seriously
- Married and generally happy
- Married but facing difficulties and looking for answers
- Divorcing and not happy about it
- Single parent and coping
- Single parent and looking for next marriage

All of these are personal answers, which should help you to be prepared for the study of God's Word that shows the ideal circumstances which God wants to give and to which you undoubtedly want to achieve.

*What are your personal prayers and hopes for your relationship in your own personal family? (This answer is private.)*

**Week Twelve**                                                    **243**

## Day One -- Male and Female Genders

The love of a man and woman which leads to marriage was God's idea.  Sexuality is woven into the very creation of human beings.  Genesis shows that God deliberately created "male and female" (Gen. 1:27).  After having created man from dust, God formed a woman from Adam's rib, and He Himself "brought her to the man" (Gen. 2:22).

The Bible shows that God created the sexual capabilities for intimacy, bonding and procreation.  The sexual relationship was intended to bring a man and woman closer together, provide an intense emotional tie, and enable them to give birth to children and thus perpetuate the race.  God had a purpose for the sexual relationship for the first couple: *"God blessed them and said to them, "Be fruitful and increase in number; fill the earth and subdue it"*(Gen. 1:28 ff). *"For this reason a man will leave his father and mother and be united to his wife, and they will become one flesh"(Gen. 2:24).*

***What is the beauty of God's plan related to maleness and femaleness?  What do the above offer in answer to this question?***

Married love is intended to be personal, warm, caring, intimate, sensitive, joyous, intelligent, purposeful and meaningful to both partners, not impersonal, mechanical, exploitative or abusive.

Marriage succeeds only when done God's way.  It exists for the sake of service to God and His people.  It functions best in the context and support of Christian community. A foundation to understanding marriage is a proper view of male and female.

None of us is merely a person, for each of us has a gender. The distinctiveness of being male or female reaches to the very core of our identity. Whatever we do, we do first as a man or as a woman. Our distinction is far greater than anatomy, voice pitch, clothing and hairstyle. Gender, masculinity, and femininity, which is a vital part of the true self and personhood, is rooted in God. Men and women are made for physical, social, emotional, psychological and spiritual intimacy with each other (Gen. 2:18-25).

Uni-sex ideas come from cultural confusion that clouds our gender identities and keep us from being whole and healthy. God has polarized us into two genders, which fact should be recognized and acted on accordingly. As we possess our individual identities, we can function in a healthy manner. Giving fully what we have to give as man or woman allows us to function naturally to complement each other in marriage and in the family, as in society. It is just like using the right tool for the right job.

1.  *Explain the purpose of males and females on the basis of Prov. 31:1-3, Col. 3:18-19 and 1 Pet. 1:7? What is the character, role and function of male and female?*

2.  *How and why does society fall apart or get unbalanced when our culture gets confused about genders?*

## Day Two -- The Nature and Purpose of Marriage

God establishes order and responsibility in marriage. Someone has to be given the responsibility of spiritual leader, and God has given it to the husband (1 Cor.11:35). Christ is the head of the man, and the man is the spiritual head of the woman, as Christ is Head of the Church. The husband's headship requires commitment to his wife, and unselfish sacrifice for her. He is to be a servant with active love, nourishing, cherishing and providing for her (Eph. 5:21-25; Col. 3:18-19). Paul's teaching was based on God's command, not on his personal opinion or cultural tendencies (1 Cor. 14:37).

*Read the following Scriptures and tell the purpose of marriage.*

| | |
|---|---|
| Gen. 2:18-24 | |
| Gen. 1:28; Ps. 127:3-5 | |
| 1 Cor. 7:3-5 | |
| Eph. 6:1-4 | |

The husband first sets an example by the way he loves and respects his wife. Fathers carry the primary parental responsibility for representing God to their children. They are to protect their children spiritually, emotionally, morally, socially and physically (Prov. 19:18).

When Paul talks of headship in the home, he means spiritual authority, not authoritarian, arbitrary or dictatorial domination over a wife. This is not a military chain of command or a political bureaucracy which requires unthinking obedience,

**Week Twelve** 246

but it is a sensitive and delicate love relationship, like the pattern of Christ loving His Church, and the Church obeying Christ.

Christ is our example, both in subordinating Himself to the Father on His earthly mission and as Head of the Church.  He did not please Himself, but pleased the Father (Romans 15:3).

*What do we learn about husband-wife relationships in these verses?*

| Phil. 2:5-8 | |
| --- | --- |
| Eph. 5:21 | |

The husband is to fulfill his duty to his wife (1 Cor. 7:3) and give up his authority over his own body and not to defraud her (1 Cor. 7:4-5).  The wife, on the other hand, is to fulfill her duty to her husband (1 Cor. 7:3) and also to give up her authority over her own body.  This does not mean subjection or subordination to the male, but being subject spiritually to him as the Church is subject to Christ.

The husband first sets an example by the way he loves and respects his wife.  Fathers carry the primary parental responsibility for representing God to their children.  Fathers are the main source for personal identity for children to be Christ-like.  They must provide love and discipline (Rom. 11:22).  Any change of function in male or female or in husband or wife is a deviation from the Biblical direction of our very being and of our created order. Attempts at change of functions arise because of our sinful nature and worldly desire.  Since the Fall, all men and women struggle in this matter.

The Scriptures have not shortchanged women by giving them the less desirable roles of submissive "helpmates" and nurturers while the men have the more desirable positions of

**Week Twelve**                                                    **247**

leaders and providers. Any discussion of desirable roles reflect our society's values more than that of the Scriptures. There is no replacing the wife or mother any more than replacing the husband or father.

*1. How is the family benefited when the husband accepts the role as spiritual head/servant of the home? To what is this headship limited?*

*2. What is the role of a wife in a Christian marriage? How is the home benefited when the wife accepts this role?*

*3. How can a husband and wife build a strong marriage?*

Being single can also be God's gift. Paul spoke openly about being single, and he even made a strong statement, "It's good for men not to get married...I say to those who are not married, especially to widows: It is good to you to stay single like me. However, if you cannot control your desires, you should get married. It is better for you to marry than to burn with sexual desire"(1 Cor. 7:1, 8:9). Singleness is a fact of life with a good number of men and an even greater number of women.

Whether being single is a decision or an involuntary act, singles should make their singleness as positive an experience as possible, as they conduct themselves morally on the basis of Christian principles. Paul describes the single condition in very

**Week Twelve**                                    248

positive terms, giving insights that can help single people live happily and productively.  Though the Bible is strongly weighted in favor of marriage and the family,  Paul's teaching must put singles completely at ease.  Without  requiring us to make comparisons between marriage and singleness, he states that both are good.  So Paul makes singleness not the opposite of marriage, but rather an alternative to marriage, and an honorable status.

*If you are single, describe your hopes for companionship relating either to marriage or to friendships.  If you are married, tell how you want to bring more singles into your circle of friendships.*


Go to God in prayer and ask Him to help you make a positive impact on your immediate family and your extended family, whether single or married.  After your time of prayer, spend a minute in silence.  Record any thoughts you might have below.


## Day Three -- Keeping the Peace/Handling Conflicts in Families

When sin entered human sexual identity, people began to compensate in one way or another. When males become aware of their weaknesses, they sometimes counteract by emphasizing whatever they like in themselves or they generate a counterfeit sense of masculinity through aggression, rebellion and

exaggerated independence.  In some cases, they retreat passively
to demand that others take care of them.

Females quickly feel violated and unsafe if their trust has
been betrayed.  At that time, they feel shame and fear which is
attached to the loss of their full  identity.  Then, males lack the
healthy confidence that they are fully male, while females lack
assurance that they are secure women.

When roles are confused, men pursue defensive strategies
to compensate and so dominate their families or neglect them.
Women exaggerate their physical appeal, while some become
docile and accept the demeaning control of someone who will take
care of them.

*How may God's divine purpose for marriage be harmed or
destroyed?*

Problems erupt when family members try to buy love or
control and manipulate others with things.  Problems which are
normal will enlarge and become a cause of conflict and a family
fight.  Rather than comforting one another in failures, mistakes,
and losses, they will emphasize the weaknesses of others while
gloating over their own innocence.

Unhealthy families have many negative qualities which
need attention and correction.  Individual members are isolated
and out of touch with others in the unhealthy family.  They are
rigid and talk mostly about events and things rather than
communicating love and concern about each other. Their love is
external or a payoff, and there is little or no trust.  They have
poorly defined or no boundaries or expectations.  There are
denials and lies, but not the truth.  They are co-dependent,
whereas healthy families are interdependent.

**Week Twelve**                                                  250

*1. What are the main causes of conflict in families?*

*2. How can individual members of the family keep peace?*

God wants marriage to last for a lifetime. Thus, divorce is marriage failure or missing the marital target. Matthew 19:3-12, referring to the Law in Deuteronomy 24:1-4, quotes Jesus in the principle that divorce is wrong. Paul provides a lengthy discourse on marriage, marital difficulties and divorce in 1 Corinthians 7:1-16. The only reason for divorce is unfaithfulness or desertion. When it occurs, repentance and forgiveness are to be sought so that the offending party may be restored as a healthy member of the Christian community.

*1. How can a husband and wife avoid divorce?*

*2. How do extra-marital affairs destroy the family?*

Homosexual marriages are a gross sin and are forbidden (1 Cor. 6:9; Rom. 1:27).

*What should the church say or do concerning homosexuality?*

**Week Twelve**

Living in repentance and forgiveness in Christ is the only liberating power for men to be strong and tender in properly representing Christ, for women to be secure and giving, both living out God's design.  The direction of our spiritual lives will help to solve whatever difficulties there are in marriages and families.

Go to God in prayer and thank Him for the good relations you have in marriage or as a single, and then ask Him to show you and help you to have better relations and companionship. After your time of prayer, spend a minute in silence.  Record any thoughts you might have below.

## Day Four -- Turning Marriages Into Families, and Houses Into Homes

God wants to bless the world through Christian families. His aim, authority and glory are to be communicated through the family.  The "church in your house" was a central factor in early New Testament Christianity.  Society and the church are only as strong as their families and homes.

One of the best blueprints for the Christian home is found in Ephesians 5 and 6: 1. a right relationship with God; 2. walking in love and abstaining from evil; 3. spending time with God through worship, Bible study and prayer; 4. being empowered by the Holy Spirit; 5. keeping father, mother and children in high regard; 6. being bonded together through meaningful, loving and honest commitment to God's Word.

*What good counsel do we receive from:*

| Heb. 12:3-11 | |
|---|---|
| Prov. 19:18 | |

When God's Word and the church influence in making proper family choices and decisions, then TV, videos and VCRs, friends, culture and other forces will not be a negative force, tearing the family apart.   Taking Christian communication seriously, the Christian home should be a nurturing center where a family of Christian priests enjoy each other and feed faithfully on the Word.

There are more basic family functions and needs than protection, economic security, education and status.  The most important functions of a family are  relational, providing love, nurture, and care.   Individuals cannot be healthy where unconditional love and nurturing are not supplied. The family breaks down when its members search elsewhere for loving and helpful relations.

*What makes the home a "haven of grace and love?"*

The healthy family helps members to discover God and commit themselves to Him.  It also provides godly role models, establishes clear rules and boundaries for the family's security and protection, and applies these equally to every individual. Appropriate consequences that are consistent and fair are

**Week Twelve**                                                  253

established for violating rules.  Trust and openness are developed.
There will be celebration of one another's joys, accomplishments
or hurts, always giving encouragement and positive
reinforcement.

*1.  What is a healthy family?*


*2.  How can a marriage be turned into a family and a house
into a home?*


Christian parents should seek to make their home a
school for learning the essentials about relationships with Christ
and fellow men.  The home should also be a hospital where loving
care and healing are given to wounded members of their family.
It should also be an evangelism center where non-Christian
friends and neighbors feel welcome and experience the love with
which Christ has enriched the family.

Single parent families, as well as single individuals, are a
reality.  Their homes must be permeated with the same Christian
influence which makes houses into homes.  Singleness is an
alternative to marriage (Matt. 19:12).  Whether a single person or
a single parent, there should be devotion to the kingdom of God
and living positively and productively.

*What do we learn about singleness in 1 Cor. 7:1, 8-9, 17?*


**Week Twelve**                                      **254**

Go to God in prayer and ask Him to make you an influence to turn marriages into families, and houses into homes. After your time of prayer, spend a minute in silence. Record any thoughts you might have below.


## Day Five -- My Community and World Family

The same Biblical principles that apply to relations in the family should apply in relations with others, including between individuals of different ethnic or racial heritage. The racial problem is primarily a moral and spiritual one. God created all nations and ethnic backgrounds from one person (Acts 17:26).

*What do the following Bible verses tell us about human relations and the treatment people are to give each other?*

| | |
|---|---|
| Luke 10:30-37<br>John 4:30 | |
| Gen. 1:27 | |
| Acts 17:26 | |
| Rom. 3:23<br>Col. 3:11 | |
| Matt. 16:26 | |

*Thinking about the Gospel content of Rev. 14:6 and Ps. 33:5, how does the Gospel dynamic solve human relations problems, including family and race?*


**Week Twelve**                                    **255**

Christ set an example in life dealings with others in His relations with the Samaritans. He made a "good Samaritan" the hero of one of His parables. When the Samaritan woman reminded Jesus that He was a Jew and she was a Samaritan, and that Jews do not associate with Samaritans, Jesus showed again that there is to be no segregation or prejudice between races.

Love for God and neighbor of whatever race is commanded by Christ (Matt. 22:34-40). Jesus destroyed the "we-you" attitude which is at the root of many racial and human problems. When the Jews tried to claim to be blue bloods as Abraham's descendants (John 8:33), Jesus shattered their pious religious traditions by exposing their bigoted slavery to religious rules against the freedom of the Gospel.

*What do we learn about human relations from:*

| Gen. 43:31-32 | |
| --- | --- |
| Acts 10:28 | |
| John 4:9 | |
| Luke 10:30-37 | |
| Acts 11:1-18 | |

Paul asserted clearly that we are all from the same source and one family stock, and related to God (Acts 17:26-28). We differ in complexion, customs and culture, but we are brothers and sisters in the human family under God. Peter reinforced this when he said that God does not play favorites (Acts 10:34-35).

God's attitude toward all people is to be the basis of our human relationships.

Prejudice against another person is always wrong, for it shows a pride of importance and worth by considering others unimportant. Prejudice allows people to feel like winners by forcing other people down. The Christian community demonstrates that the categories of winners and losers are an evil result of our sinful culture.

Our relationship to each other means that we are not made for ourselves alone. Bigotry, segregation, prejudice and exclusiveness are seen in God's Word as a denial of faith. Hostile attitudes toward another deny the wholeness of a person, which God desires. Nothing in the Bible, anthropology or sociology warrants any kind of bigotry or racism. God commands the positive action of seeking justice, stopping oppression, defending orphans and pleading the case of widows (Is. 1:17).

Christians must see prejudice as a sin, while pointing to Jesus who loved the sinner as an example of our love. When we show love to people who experience partiality, we undermine the security that feeds the prejudice. Our love drives out intolerance in others.

*1.   What words and actions are inconsistent with or contrary to color-blind Christian love?*

*2.   What should Christians do to overcome racial prejudice or bigotry in their community and nation?*

3. *Why is it difficult to recognize racial prejudice within ourselves?*

4. *Go to God in prayer and ask Him to identify racial intolerance and prejudice among people who are in your circle of influence, even yourself. Pray that God will remove these injustices and empower all to show love. After your time of prayer, spend a minute in silence. Record any thoughts you might have below.*

## OBSERVATIONS/REFLECTIONS ON WHAT YOU STUDIED THIS WEEK:

1. What matters or issues would you like to know more about? What, if anything, troubled you about what you studied?

2. What new knowledge or insights have you learned?

3. How has your faith grown or been modified?

4. How will this affect your life?

**Week Twelve**

# WEEK THIRTEEN

# MANAGING MY LIFE FOR GOD

How can we live with our resources without them owning and controlling us? We are to have no other god's before God. Our "gods" are not always obvious to us. Satan is smart. He puts many things in our lives that become objects of excessive attachment. This ends in worshipping these "gods" instead of the one true God. The pursuit of these "gods" continues endlessly because they bring no lasting satisfaction.

*Look around your neighborhood. What evidence do you see that would indicate many people are busy chasing after things? Do you think they see these things as "gods"? Why or why not?*

As Christians, how can we avoid worshipping things instead of God? How can we truly love God and serve Him only? The key to understanding this matter is in how we view our role as human beings. Are we here simply to consume or are we here to manage? Understanding the depth of God's plan and provision for all of our needs also points us to God's answer.

God has made us His representatives to manage all creation. Living in this recognition places God first above all things where we can't confuse the created with the Creator. God commanded human beings as the crown of His creation to subdue and multiply what He gave them to manage. God placed us under Himself as the Supplier.

**Week Thirteen**                                        259

Managers of God's creation is an accurate job description for Christians.  Management is God's call for people to care for, nurture, and love their home, Earth.  Planet Earth, and all that it supplies, has been entrusted to us for loving care.  All creatures are dependent upon the complex ecological system of the earth for clean food, air, water and living space.  As wonderful as the earth is, we are not to worship any part of the creation.  The assignment to manage, have dominion and control is part of God's call to righteousness and holy living.  We are not just  "passing through" on our way to heaven.  We are God's partners and managers in what God has given.

## Day One -- Godly Management or Consumerism

God told Adam and Eve that they were to manage everything except one tree, which He reserved for Himself.  He left them to manage the earth and its creatures.  Then Satan, the "master consumer," focused on the one tree reserved for God's management.  He motivated Adam and Eve to go selfishly beyond the management responsibilities which God had given them.

Satan deceived Adam and Eve to believe that God's supply was inadequate or that His plan was flawed.  Now they became possessors and accumulators, taking control for themselves instead of managing for God and suffering the consequence.

*What consequences do you see as a result of the world's emphasis on  possessing and accumulating instead of managing for God?*

God sent Adam and Eve out of the garden into the human wasteland of consumerism.   As a result all of humankind is involved in this struggle of weeds and land, cut throat economy, competitive industry, and dehumanizing technology with bruised relationships. Only Christians who follow God's plan can help the world see godly management instead of selfish consumerism. The problem is Christians often behave just like their materialistic non-Christian counterparts.

*What decisions may you have made in your life that reflect a misunderstanding of your role as God's partner?*

| Area of Your Life | Example of Your Misunderstanding |
| --- | --- |
| Financial resources | |
| Skills and Abilities | |
| Time | |

Materialism is the gaining of resources as the greatest goal of life while ignoring relationships. Often our relationship with God is the first thing sacrificed. Consumerism finds man using selfishly for himself that which he is to manage for God. This is defiance against God, another reason our relationship with God suffers in consumerism. Such selfishness once became so great that God destroyed all creatures except Noah's family and those in the ark by a flood (Gen. 6 and 7).

Consumerism is the using of goods that has gone wild, a turning into ourselves rather than managing our resources for the good of all. Materialism and consumerism are a deformed view of property and the world which plead, "Buy, purchase, own." It tells us we will feel better if we own more. It tells us that our identity is tied to what we possess.

God's people, Israel, frequently perverted God's gracious plan for their task to care for the earth and its creatures. He had set them as managers for the good of all (Jer. 1:10). Their

**Week Thirteen** 261

consumer mentality and ways brought God's anger (Haggai 1:3-7, 11). As managers, the people of Israel failed to see their role in God's plan and the effect of disobedience on their lives. Israel ultimately paid a great price for their mismanagement. Their kingdom was dismantled, and they were exiled to other lands. We can avoid this peril by living in accordance to God's management plan. Placing God's plan first ensures our well being and advances His kingdom through our resources.

We see the devil approaching Jesus as he did Adam and Eve in order to get consumerism to prevail. He took Jesus to a high mountain and showed him the splendor of all the kingdoms of the world and said that he would give Jesus all this if Jesus would worship him. The devil tried to gain Jesus as the king of consumerism of the new era, but Jesus resisted. Satan approaches each of us with the same questions, offering things in place of God. Answering incorrectly propels us into an endless cycle of spending, working hard to pay for it, becoming dissatisfied only to spend more, and start the cycle over again. How can we break Satan's grip?

**Which of the following feelings best describes your attitude toward material things?**

- *Material things are important indicators of my position in life.*
- *I'm afraid of the prospect of losing material possessions.*
- *I find comfort in the power I have to purchase what I want.*
- *I am having difficulty letting go of the importance of possessions.*

*How has this attitude affected your ability to live according to God's plan for us as managers?*

If we don't manage all of God's resources for the good of all and for use in Christ's mission, we will fall into the trap of worshipping things as our gods.  We bring nothing to God as we receive forgiveness, love and faith.  That is God's value system which contradicts the human system of consumerism, position, greed and piracy.

If all we have accomplished in our earthly life is success, collectibles, leisure and education, then we have not honored God.  Our lives should be lived in the recognition of God as owner, while we are His administrators.  We must honestly ask ourselves how much importance we are placing on "things" and how we are to use what we have for the promotion of God's kingdom on earth.

Go to God now and ask Him to show you areas of your life where you are more a consumer than a manager.  Ask Him to show you those things that are objects of  excessive attachment and free you from their grip.  After your time of prayer spend a minute in silence.  Record any thoughts you might have below.

## Day Two -- Christians are God's Channels

Christians are God's channels, chosen to serve and to be equipped for mission.  But the world and our old nature present the choice of human consumerism rather than godly management as channels for God.  God made us custodians, not owners.  Jesus said we cannot serve both God and possessions (Matt. 24).

1.  *Why is it difficult for us to be content with what we have? How much is enough?*

*Week Thirteen*

2.	*What attitudes and practices in our life and culture discourage us from being God's channels?*

Our Christian faith sets us as channels of God in His hand and providence.  As God's channels, we give ourselves to serve.  Our faith challenges the self-oriented values of our society and calls us to abandon self-centered lives and value systems. Our faith causes us to recognize and confess God as Lord/Creator of the universe with ourselves as managers. God promises us that we can meet the challenge of becoming His channel on earth.

There is nothing wrong with us having things, for God has given us the good things to use and enjoy.  The Bible does not condemn the possession of material things, for it recognizes a place in everyone's life for enjoying things.  It recognizes no purpose for abundance other than a means of serving God and our fellow men.  God always values people more than possessions, and tells people not to covet and not to be greedy, but to be satisfied with what they have.  He forbids waste and careless destruction of His resources.

James warned people who make possessions and money their security and "god," wanting more than they need: *"Your wealth has rotted, and moths have eaten your clothes...and you have lived on earth in luxury and self-indulgence.  You have fattened yourselves in the day of slaughter"*(James 5:2, 5).

The true and living God warns people against treating material goods as if they were really gods.  Instead of people's temporary happiness going on forever, they will reap and weep for the miseries that are coming upon them.  These warnings are important because our work and money are tied and interrelated to the significance of creation and God's providence.  The

**Week Thirteen**	264

question is how we can maintain our balance in the outrageous extremes we see in materialism and consumerism. Through these excesses, we turn good into bad, eating into gluttony, sex into adultery, and relationships into pain and competition.

We have accumulated things, but have alienated ourselves from people. We have become slaves of our possessions and technology. Hands that push buttons, throw switches and steer wheels have lost considerably the ability to lovingly touch, care, defend, plant and reap. They are designed to be God's channels.

As God's channels, we follow God's system of working, earning, providing charity, caring, helping and loving as individual disciples and as a Christian community. Our ability to carry out God's system depends on where we place our values. Study the list of values below. Select the one you would rank first in your present lifestyle. Continue the process until you have a complete rank ordering of all twelve values.

*What's Important To Me?*

| Value | Priority | Value | Priority |
| --- | --- | --- | --- |
| Wealth, being prosperous | | Security for my family | |
| Accomplishment | | Doing the will of God | |
| Recognition and admiration | | Power | |
| Resolving inner conflict | | Closeness with other | |
| Enjoying life | | Equality with others | |
| Happiness | | Safety | |

Go to your Father in Heaven now in prayer and ask Him to help you see clearly how your value system must change so that you can become His channel of love and grace to the world. Read 2 Cor. 9:10-13. What promise is God offering us? After your time of prayer spend a minute in silence. Record any thoughts you might have below.

## Day Three -- Representatives and Priests of God

God's chosen people in the Old and New Testaments are called priests. As priest, we have some very specific duties.

*What are Christian priests and what are they to do?*

| | |
|---|---|
| Exodus 19:5-6 | |
| 1 Peter 2:9 | |

God's priests are **to go to God for people, and to go to people for God.** People are the most precious resources on earth. We do not abandon our daily work in order to spend all our time to perform sacred rituals in church, but as God's royal priests, we take the sacred to the secular, sharing the love of Christ in our daily work and life.

"Going to God for people" means that we pray for ourselves, family, neighbors, friends, community, nation and the entire world. We intercede for them that God's saving grace and providence will be provided everywhere to all either directly or through us as God's managers.

"Going to people for God" means that we are God's representatives or priests as part of the Christian community are involved in meeting spiritual and material needs wherever they

**Week Thirteen** 266

may be found. We do not live merely to accumulate resources, but to utilize them in order to live profitably as His managers for the good of all.  We are to love and serve each other in the entire human family.  God has given us abundant resources so that we may be generous as we go to people for God.

"Going to people for God" also means that we are ready to share our lives with others in a way that they can clearly see the Word at work in all that we do. Rather than being called out of our work to sit in church, we are called from church to our work in the world.  Everyone is called to this full-time job of sharing the Word in homes, in neighborhoods and at work.


*In what ways can you act as God's priest in your daily life:*

- *Go to God for people?*



- *Go to people for God?*



Our homes and our jobs are all extensions of God's work. They are the settings of our priesthood activities.  Because of our sin, none of our work completely fulfills God's intentions, but this does not take away from the dignity of the roles that God has assigned us.  Under God's authority as priests and disciples, we exercise our privilege to influence His whole creation through the careful use of His resources to share Christ's love.

*"Whatever you do, work at it with all your heart, as working for the Lord, not for men, since you know that you will receive*

*an inheritance from the Lord as a reward. It is the Lord Christ you are serving"* (Col. 3:23-24).

Go to God now in prayer and ask Him to show you more clearly how your entire existence should be evaluated in light of your priestly duties. Ask Him for an understanding of one thing that you can do this week for each of these priestly activities:

- Going to God for people
- Going to people for God

After your time of prayer spend a minute in silence. Record any thoughts you might have below.

## Day Four -- God's Servants

Jesus, the divine picture of a servant, said, *"...I am among you as one who serves"* (Luke 22:24). Only the servant model of Jesus in His life and work can be fully adequate for the stewardship of our lives. Jesus also said, *"Whoever serves Me must follow Me...My Father will honor the one who serves Me"* (John 12:26).

Servanthood is the basic model for the normal Christian life. Jesus defined the servant in this way: "...Whoever wants to become great among you must be your servant, and whoever wants to be first must be your slave...just as the Son of Man did not come to be served, but to serve, and to give His life as a ransom for many"(Matt. 20:26-28). Members of the church are not only to be served, but to be servants themselves. We are not just to perform acts of service, but to be servants. We are not to be spiritual sponges which absorb teaching and doctrine, but disciples of Christ to offer unselfish service in servanthood. We are not to strive for service positions and recognition, but to seek

**Week Thirteen** 

places to serve joyously with our God-given abilities. Being servants is the support system required for those hurting in Christ's body and in the world.

*Why are people content to absorb teaching and not serve?*

A servant is one who sacrifices self-interest for self-extension in which concern for others balances with concern for oneself. This comes from sacrificial love, which is an essential characteristic of the servant. *"Therefore, I urge you, brothers, in view of God's mercy, to offer your bodies as living sacrifices, holy and pleasing to God-- this is your spiritual act of worship"*(Rom. 12:1).

Is God asking too much? Is He unrealistic? Not if we are growing in our understanding of the great gift God has given us through Christ. The more we understand how freely God's gift of salvation is offered and how precious this gift is to us, the more motivated we are to let God change us. He is asking that our whole life is to be lived for God and that Christ dwell in us. God's plan depends on us being a part of a Christian community supporting each other by the ministry and service we give through our abilities and daily work.

*What is the full role and work of Christians as servants to others?*

Go to God in prayer and ask Him to show you the importance of servanthood. Be willing to act on the opportunities

**Week Thirteen**                                           269

God presents them to you. After your time of prayer, spend a minute in silence. Record any thoughts you might have below.

## Day Five -- Recognizing Our Spiritual Gifts

Paul said, "Now about spiritual gifts, brothers, I do not want you to be ignorant"(1 Cor. 12:1). Are you knowledgeable about spiritual gifts? The nature of God's call requires that God's people understand spiritual gifts. The church is believers functioning together according to their unique God-given gifts and ministering to each other in love.

Paul's most extensive discussion of spiritual gifts is in 1 Corinthians 12-14. Turn to chapters 12-14 and read them now.

*According to 1 Cor. 12:7 why does God give every Christian a spiritual gift?*

Paul stresses in Ephesians 4:1-16 the unity of the church in which spiritual gifts are to be used to foster fellowship and oneness. The ascended Christ, who has great riches, gives gifts to His people as He desires (Eph. 4:7). God gives specific gifts to specific persons for specific purposes. These gifts are given to equip or prepare disciples for their work of service or ministry to build up the body of Christ.

There is a great diversity of spiritual gifts, but a unity in the Body to serve one another for the common good. The use of spiritual gifts is governed by our life purpose of proclaiming the Gospel and salvation to sinners. All gifts must be used to build up the body of Christ in such a manner that it does not violate or disrupt good order which God expects in the church.

Peter summarizes: *"Each one should use whatever gift he has received to serve others, faithfully administering God's grace in its various forms"*(1 Peter 4:10). Peter states that every Christian has received some spiritual gift, which is not his or hers to use or bury or use as they please.

Spiritual gifts are God's way of getting His work done in the world through the church. They are a key to His ministry through people. All authority and direction for their use come from Christ, our Head. There are dangers in their use by pride and of counterfeiting of them. Misuse causes confusion, strife and jealousy. Abuses of spiritual gifts include ignoring them, refusing to use them, insisting that all should have a specific gift, exalting one gift over another, or failing to realize that all gifts come from God.

Various written "tests" have been developed that may be helpful in identifying your gifts. Whether you take a test or not, you should begin serving others. This step will allow others to affirm your spiritual gifts. Follow these simple steps:

1. Ask God in prayer to show you your gifts. Read and reread the Scriptures listed below and the descriptions of the gifts.
2. Experiment. Try performing various acts of ministry within the safety of a small group. Ask for feedback. Examine how you feel, but don't let the voice of fear drown out affirmation you might get from other people.
3. Watch for things to happen. Are people responding to the ministry you are doing?

Christians do not call themselves to specific responsibilities, but are called through the church. The Body is empowered to call members to service and to help them identify their gifts. Our church offers many opportunities to explore giftedness through a variety of ministries and training. In this way, God does His work through the church by giving believers spiritual gifts and abilities to do His work.  It is vital that everyone discovers and uses their spiritual gifts.

1.   *How are Christians a key to God's ministry to people?*

2.   *How should care be taken in the use of Spiritual gifts? How may we be tempted to abuse this matter?*

Go to God now in prayer and ask Him to help you be bold in ministry so that you might be affirmed in your spiritual gift(s).  Pray that you will use your gift to its fullest for the glory of Christ and the good of the church.  After your time of prayer, spend a minute in silence.  Record any thoughts you might have below.

## Major Points to Review

1.   *How do you struggle with managing all that you have for God's purpose rather than your purpose?*

2.   *After ranking your values on page 265, what steps should you take to reorder them?*

**Week Thirteen**                                        

3. *How can you reorder your life so that you may carry out your priestly duties?*

4. *What step could you take this week to begin serving another person, if you are not serving others regularly?*

5. *What ministry could you take on within your group that would give you a chance to affirm an area of giftedness?*

## OBSERVATIONS/REFLECTIONS ON WHAT YOU STUDIED THIS WEEK

1. What matters or issues would you like to know more about?  What, if anything, troubled you about what you studied?

2. What new knowledge or insights have you learned?

3. How has your faith grown or been modified?

4. How will this affect your life?

**Week Thirteen** 273

# WEEK FOURTEEN

# MANAGING MY LIFE FOR CHRIST

## Day One -- Using my Abilities

In 1988 a study was completed by the University of Michigan with 2700 older people over a ten year period to determine the impact of volunteer work and service to others on people's health. Those who performed regular volunteer work had a dramatic increase of life expectancy. People who did not perform volunteer work were 2 ½ times more likely to die during this time than those who did some service at least once a week. Those who were turned in to themselves were similarly less healthy than those who looked out from themselves to serve others. Reacting to this, a prominent psychologist said that in view of these findings, wise doctors should consider a prescription of service and volunteer work for their patients for gaining health.

We human beings are part of a social family planned by God to be dependent upon each other by services we give through our abilities and daily work. Christians have been given special abilities to use for others in the body of Christ, Who is our model.

*What is your reaction to the University of Michigan research results?*

Many Christians seem to have a spiritual inferiority complex, ignorant of their great assets and resources while being too aware of their weaknesses and liabilities.  The result is a sense of worthlessness and weakness in living for and serving the Resurrected Christ.

There is no Christian, unless limited by disabilities,  who has not been gifted somehow for God's service, strengthened by the Holy Spirit.  Paul said, "Therefore, my dear brothers, stand firm.  Let nothing move you.  Always give yourselves fully to the work of the Lord, because you know that your labor in the Lord is not in vain"(1 Cor. 15:58).  Also, "Serve wholeheartedly, as if you were serving the Lord, not men"(Eph. 6:7).

*What did Jesus say related to our call to Christian service in:*

| Matt. 21:28 | |
|---|---|
| Mark 13:34 | |

Some accountants use an interesting device known as a T. On one side of the T are listed assets - things owned such as a home, car, etc.  On the other side are liabilities or debts - what is owed.  Then each column is totaled. If the liabilities exceed the assets, there must be a correction.

We will be benefited by doing a periodic T-Account of ourselves as we list our assets and  abilities and gifts, and then list in the other column how we are using them.  How do we balance on each side of the T regarding abilities and service?  Are there too many liabilities because of fear, doubts and negative thinking?

Through our self-evaluation, we can be led to establish priorities to use our abilities that are not being used for God at this time.  Why not make an audit of ourselves to study what we are doing with our personal resources - using them for God, totally for ourselves or a balance between God and us?

*Make a T-Account of your own abilities and use of them.*

**Week Fourteen**

275

True joy as a Christian is not being where you want to be, doing what you want to do, but being where God wants you to be and doing what God wants you to do.

1. *How can we become more aware of the gifts God has given us?*

2. *What kind of service do you hope to give to God and the church in the future?*

Go to God and thank Him for the abilities and spiritual gifts He has given you and ask Him to enlarge your opportunities to glorify Christ and to serve Him in physical and spiritual need. After your time of prayer, spend a minute in silence. Record any thoughts you might have below.

## Day Two – Prioritizing My Time

Paul gives good advice on time management: "Be very careful, then, how you live - not as unwise, but as wise, making the most of every opportunity, for the days are evil"(Eph. 5:15-16). The primary consideration in use of time is the will of God, living harmoniously with the plan God has for us.

**Week Fourteen**                                                   276

*What lessons about time did Jesus teach in:*

| Luke 2:49 | |
|---|---|
| John 4:34 | |
| John 9:4 | |
| John 17:4 | |

Jesus showed the value, limit and brevity of time: "As long as it is day, I must do the work of Him who sent Me. Night is coming, when no one can work"(Jn. 9:4). He showed the best use of time: "My food is to do the will of Him who sent Me, and to finish His work"(Jn. 4:34). He showed the reward of time: "I have brought You glory on earth by completing the work You gave Me to do"(Jn. 17:4).

*What does Paul teach us about time in:*

| 1 Cor. 7:29-31 | |
|---|---|
| Rom. 13:11-14 | |

Everyone has the same amount of time day by day. But some have long lives and some have short lives. Time cannot be saved, stored, stretched or stopped for a future date. Time never takes time off. No one really has enough time. People can usually find ways to save time.

God expects good management of time, and it is possible. We are accountable individually for the use of our time. It is important to determine God's timetable for us. We need to

**Week Fourteen** 277

distinguish between God's time and our time.  Our time can be lost by a lack of clear goals and commitment and by our own procrastination and excuses for not being on time.

Because there is meaning and purpose to life, it does make a difference how we use our time.  We should have a sense of time, but not be slaves of time.  It is especially meaningful when it presents a special opportunity, like harvest time or the right time.

We must recognize **time robbers**, such as TV, videos, overindulgence in spectator sports, and purposeless socializing.

*1.   What are some of our misplaced priorities?*


*2.   What are some of the biggest time robbers in our lives?*


Priorities for the use of time are:
1.   Time with God for meditation and Bible study
2.   Time with your family
3.   Time for yourself for quiet meditation
4.   Time with the body of Christ
5.   Time for work
6.   Time with other people
7.   Time to plan
8.   Time for recreation
9.   Time for rest and relaxation.
     Suggestions for managing our time are:
1.   Decide what we want to do with our lives and set our goals accordingly

**Week Fourteen**                                    

2. Establish priorities for using our time based on that plan
3. Change whatever habits need changing to achieve those goals
4. Have a desire to use time according to God's will
5. Pray that God will help us overcome bad time management habits
6. Set deadlines and do not procrastinate.

We will be wise to heed God's will: "Whatever your hand finds to do, do it will all your might, for in the grave, where you are going. There is neither working nor planning nor knowledge nor wisdom"(Ecc. 9:10). When we are wise time managers, it will be because we have determined that every day will be a day of growth in knowledge and wisdom to be stronger in our Christian faith.

Christ is glorified when at the end of each day we call tell God or write a journal which records that we have consciously tried to glorify God in each of our actions, and sign our name.

*What is the difference between God's time and man's time? How should a Christian try to get his time in line with God's time?*

Go to God in prayer and tell Him of your commitment placing your life and your time in His hands and at the end of each day that Christ may be glorified. After your time of prayer, spend a minute in silence. Record any thoughts you might have below.

## Day Three – My Body and Health

Our bodies are temples of the Holy Spirit (1 Cor. 6:19). As we recognize the human body as a precious resource for productivity and enjoyment in life, we will establish priorities and balance for maintaining health and strength to serve God and fellow man. God tells us in 1 Cor. 10:31 that whether we eat or drink, or whatever we do, we should do everything to the glory of God.

*What do we learn from 1 Cor. 6:13, 19?*

There are five dimensions that are the foundation for health: nutritional awareness, physical fitness, stress management, environmental sensitivity, and self-responsibility.

Christians should learn how to be healthy, practicing good habits and giving up harmful ones. We should respond to our body's warning signs before something serious happens. When our body is kept strong and well-nourished to be able to resist disease, we have more energy and endurance, and spend less time feeling tired or being ill.

Good nutrition ordinarily determines good health. We need to care for our bodies through exercise and rest. We can expect physical problems if we overeat, drink too much, overwork, underexercise, wrongly use God's gift of sex, and smoke tobacco and use dangerous substances. We can cause many illnesses by not living responsibly and not regarding our bodies as the dwelling place of the Holy Spirit.

*What do you consider to be the main principles for achieving good health?*

**Week Fourteen**                                        280

Discipline and moderation are the key.  A change of attitude which leads to a change in life style is good for our health.  Good health habits promote the quality and length of life which God wants us to enjoy.

Contributing to ill health, physical weaknesses and cardiac problems are caffeine, alcohol, intoxicants, and tobacco. In view of Biblical principles of health, it seems appropriate that Christians should refrain from these substances which are harmful.

Since God is the Giver of life and health, the Christian will earnestly seek to avoid doing whatever needlessly destroys, harms, decreases or endangers health and life.  Since God in love created, redeemed, and regenerated us in order that we might live for Him and our fellow man, the Christian will earnestly endeavor to avoid whatever hinders him in service or reduces his time on earth.

*What ways can we harm our bodies?*

Christ's disciples should establish good eating habits, exercise regularly, avoid unnecessary stimulants, get enough sleep and let their Christian faith give them strong and healthy emotions which help them avoid everything that is injurious.

*How does the Fifth Commandment relate to over-indulgences, smoking, and use of alcohol?*

Go to God in prayer and ask Him for strength to rearrange your habits and priorities related to your body and health.  After your time of prayer, spend a minute in silence. Record any thoughts you might have below.


### Day Four – Managing My Money

Money is an exchange for work or goods to help create the kind of life we want.  God gives us time and abilities, which can be exchanged for money.  This is important for human survival and existence.  Following proper money management principles and making responsible choices allows a person to enjoy more money and goods.

*What do the following passages tell us about possessions and money?*

| Deut. 8:18 | |
|---|---|
| Prov. 21:17 | |
| Ecc. 5:11 | |

Money is a gift from God.  He still owns it, even though we keep it in banks with our names attached and use it with checks which we sign. "When God gives any man wealth and possessions and enables him to enjoy them, to accept his lot and be happy in his work - this is a gift of God"(Ecc. 9:19).

*What does money represent to you and what should its ultimate purpose be?*

There will be a negative effect on our attitude if we believe that we are the owner of even a single possession.  When we make a total transfer of everything to God, we will find God's purpose for all we earn and gain.

*Why is it important for Christians to make a conscious transfer of the possessions they have in their name to God's ownership? How can you do it?*

The basic purposes of a money management plan are:
* to conserve the property and income we have;
* to put ourselves in control of our finances;
* to identify our financial problems;
* to  give us confidence in having our own money;
* to live more meaningfully and joyfully in managing incomes and possessions;
* to make financial adjustments whenever and wherever necessary.

Financial planning leads to developing step-by-step, where we are financially, what we have, what we need, and what we will have to do to get to wherever we want to go economically.

The love of money increases our concern and anxiety about worldly affairs since it puts our desires and hopes in the wrong place.  We should not cling to our possessions for security, but raise empty hands to God to be filled.  God cannot pour His riches into hands full with earthly trash.  Money will be our obedient servant, or it will be a cruel master.  Heb. 13:5 tells us not to love money but be happy with what we have because God said, "I will never abandon or leave you."

1.  *What are some of the major money problems that people experience?  How does this affect you?*

2.  *Why do families or individuals get into financial difficulties?*

Face squarely the fact that you can control your spending habits.  Plan in advance rather than trust the impulse of the moment.  Realize the consequences of your spending habits. Avoid debt.  If you have crippling financial obligations, take steps immediately to pay your debts.  Watch your use of credit cards.

*Using the following chart, write out a major goal in seven areas and then record how you will achieve it.*

| FINANCIAL AREA | GOAL | METHOD |
|---|---|---|
|  | What I want to accomplish | How I hope to achieve it |
| 1.  Giving to God and church (generous percentage) |  |  |
| 2.  Careful in buying and spending |  |  |
| 3.  Saving and investing |  |  |

| | | |
|---|---|---|
| 4. Getting out of debt | | |
| 5. Protecting my property income (insurance) | | |
| 6. Others (Name) | | |
| 7. Increasing income | | |

*1. Why should we make a budget or plan for spending?*

*2. What is so deadly about debts?*

*3. Why should children be taught Christian values in handling money?*

*4. What do you think of the possibility of living just a little bit lower than the level of life style you can afford?*

**Week Fourteen**                                    **285**

## Day Five – My Giving to God

Giving money to God does not come naturally because of our old nature.  It is more natural to complain that God wants our gifts of financial resources.  God's people in the Old Testament grumbled about offerings sometimes (Mal. 1:11-13).

*Why was God angry at the people of Malachi's day (Mal. 1:6-14)?*

Offerings and gifts do not take the place of a repentant heart.  God is concerned about the spiritual attitude and condition of the Christian steward, for whatever is not right in one's life needs correction when one gives a gift.  Hos. 6:6 tells us that God wants our obedience, not our sacrifice.  There is a prior condition to bringing a gift to God - the giving of one's self, giving up one's sinful habits and slavery to anything.  Jesus showed this: "If you are offering your gift at the altar and there remember that your brother has something against you, leave your gift there in front of the altar.  First go and be reconciled  to your brother, then come and offer your gift"(Matt. 5:23-24).

*What is the priority offering in the following Bible verses?*

| Isaiah 1:11-23 | |
| --- | --- |
| Micah 6:6-8 | |
| 1 Sam. 15:22 | |
| Hebrews 12:1 | |

**Week Fourteen**

| Psalm 51:16-17, 19 | |
|---|---|
| Mark 12:30-33 | |
| Matthew 5:23-24 | |

God's plan for our giving can be stated in five points:

1.  GIVE TO GOD FIRST.  Jesus said, "Seek first His kingdom and His righteousness, and all these things will be given to you as well"(Mt. 6:33).

    This answers the question, "Who comes first in our giving?"  The priority for Christian giving is higher than personal and family needs of food and clothes, for these are promised when we give to God first.  God did not say that we should first purchase food, clothes, cars, homes and all other necessities, and then Christ's kingdom will be added to us.  He said that we are to seek Him first, and all these things (food, clothes, etc.) will be ours as well.  The "God first" principle has God's promise that He will provide all our needs.  That is the key to happiness and security. Paul wrote that we are to give to God on the first day of the week (1 Cor. 16:2). Spending for physical needs does not come before giving for spiritual responsibilities. "Leftover giving" hurts the person and is an offense, grieves the Holy Spirit, hinders kingdom work, and dishonors God.

2.  GIVE A PLANNED PERCENTAGE OR PORTION OF YOUR INCOME.  Both the Old and New Testaments emphasize a portion or part to be set aside for God's work - sacred or separated for Kingdom tasks.  Proportionate giving

is the basis for the Old Testament tithing system and the key principle for New Testament giving. Proportionate giving means giving in proportion to the income we receive, whether large or small. It places the emphasis where it belongs - on giving from our income, not to budgets.

3. GIVE A GENEROUS PART OR PERCENTAGE TO GOD. As New Testament believers, we will prayerfully consider whether we will give more or less than God's people in the Old Testament - 10 cents out of each dollar. To give a small portion is contrary to the new nature in Christ and the power of the Holy Spirit. To give a generous part, 10% and more, is a true expression of the "Christ in us."

*What do you learn from 2 Cor. 9:10-13?*

4. FAITH SETS THE PERCENTAGE. 2 Cor. 4:2 tells us that Christian stewards are to be full of faith. The weaker the faith, the lower the percentage. The stronger the faith, the higher the percentage. Whatever a portion or percentage, we will ask ourselves whether that is the true measure of our faith and love. As we grow in faith, we will give a larger percentage.

5. GENEROUS GIVING IS A GRACE OR GIFT FROM GOD. Paul said, "...We want you to know about the grace that God has given the Macedonian churches. Out of the most severe trial, their overflowing joy and their extreme poverty welled up in rich generosity"(2 Cor. 8:1-2). These poor Christians were rich in giving as a result of God's grace/power.

1. *How does God's grace overcome all human arguments about giving?*

2. *Summarize the five steps of Christian giving and tell what their value is.*

YOUR COMMITMENT
*Will you take a close look at what you are giving and take a new step of faith by God's grace as you go through this exercise?*
My estimated annual income is: $__________
A tithe (10%) of this would be: $__________
My present offerings are: $__________
This amounts to an annual percentage of: __________%
I plan my percentage offering for next year to be: __________%
This will approximately amount to an annual total of: $__________
This will represent a weekly offering of about: $__________

Our Heavenly Father, or Senior Partner, is fully able to make 90% of your income kept for yourselves go much farther than if you fearfully keep 97% or 98% for yourself.

Go to God in prayer: if you are a tither or generous proportion giver, thank him for His grace; if you are not, ask Him to show you the benefit of adopting this Biblical practice, and strength to do it. After your time of prayer, spend a minute in silence. Record any thoughts you might have below.

**OBSERVATIONS/RELECTIONS ON WHAT YOU STUDIED THIS WEEK**

1. What matters or issues would you like to know more about? What, if anything, troubled you about what you studied?

2. What new knowledge or insights have you learned?

3. How has your faith grown or been modified?

4. How will this affect your life?

# WEEK FIFTEEN

# MANAGING FOR LIFE AND ETERNITY

### Day 1 -- Sharing Christ - Evangelism and Missions

All Christians have a spiritual aroma/smell which makes a fragrance to individuals and groups with whom they come into contact. "We are to God the aroma of Christ among those who are being saved and those who are perishing. To the one we are the smell of death, to the other, the fragrance of life"(2 Cor. 2:15-16). We should be an irresistible influence for the Gospel. It is our nature as Christians to influence others through the scent of our love.

***What is the significance of Christians being an aroma/smell?***


Jesus used several other analogies or examples to show how we should help others. One of these is salt: "You are the salt of the earth. But if the salt loses its saltiness, how can it be made salty again? It is no longer good for anything except to be thrown out and trampled by men"(Mt. 5:13). The nature and value of salt is found in its functions:

1. It is a preservative that stops spoilage of food. Likewise, we Christians are to retard and halt the decaying ways in our wicked society. Ours is a preservative role in the world.

**Week Fifteen**                                    **291**

2. The basic purpose of salt is to be seasoning for foods, to enhance or draw out its flavor. So we Christians through the Gospel should have a positive flavoring effect upon those around us.
3. Salt creates thirst. So we should live in such a manner that unbelievers will want to know why there is hope in a hopeless world.

*What is the significance of Christians being salt?*

Jesus also said, "You are the light of the world. A city on a hill cannot be hidden. Neither do people light a lamp and put it under a bowl. Instead, they put it on its stand and it gives light to every one in the house. In the same way, let your light shine before men, that they may see your good deeds and praise your Father in heaven"(Mt. 5:14-15).

Light provides visibility on the paths we walk and the ways we go. Living in a spiritually dark world, Jesus commanded us to be lights so that people may have light for their way, and see our good works and glorify our Father.

Being a light does not mean just to go to church or just to be busy in church activities. Being a light means to share the Good News of the Gospel so that our neighbors might know Christ as the Way, the Truth, and the Life. The true light is Jesus Christ. We are reflectors of that Light.

*What is the significance of Christians being Lights?*

Evangelism is not merely sharing doctrines about God, but telling about Jesus Christ and how people can have a relationship with Him. As witnessing disciples, we reflect a firsthand experience with Christ, which is the basis for our evangelism. With great compassion for the lost, we will be active in witnessing of our Savior.

*What does Acts 1:8 tell us about our witnessing assignment?*

Non-Christians may be attracted by the quality of our lives, but they need to hear the Gospel verbalized in a way that they can understand how the message relates to them. The message should be simple, not complex, and positive to reflect the reality that the Gospel is indeed Good News.

Paul tells us in 2 Tim. 1:8 not to be ashamed to tell others about our Lord. Acts 4:20 shows the urgency not to stop talking about what we have seen or heard.

Most of us enjoy talking about trips we've taken. We like to describe the scenery or places of historical significance we've visited, and the interesting things we've done. We like to show pictures, slides, or videos. We want to share our experiences with others. As salt and lights in the world, we have many opportunities to talk about our Spiritual journey with others who are having a bad trip. God gives us an opportunity to gain their interest as we share our excitement in having Jesus as our Companion.

Go to God now in prayer, and ask Him in what new ways you can be salt and a light to those around you in your circle of influence. After your time of prayer, spend a minute in silence. Record any thoughts you might have below.

**Week Fifteen**                                            **293**

## Day 2 -- Living in the Last Times

Some tend to be rather nervous about the future - perhaps even afraid -  simply because we don't know what lies ahead and wonder whether we can cope.

Before Jesus left His disciples, He told them: "I am going...to prepare a place for you...I will come back and take you to be with Me that you also may be where I am"(Jn. 14:2-3). Ever since, Christians have waited for Jesus' Second Coming at the end of time.

Jesus is coming again!  God gives Christians a serious call to be prepared for the Second Coming of Christ.  On the Last Day, "We will see the Son of Man coming in clouds with great power and glory"(Mk. 13:26).  We are traveling to the promised New Jerusalem!  We are not there merely to tour Heaven, but to be among its eternal inhabitants.  No broken asphalt or crumbling concrete roads, but streets of pure gold and gates of pearl!  Hear the marvelous sounds of angelic choirs! Face the delightful, healthful fruit of the tree of life! Dip your feet into the crystal-clear waters of the river of life! Live in the eternal presence of your heavenly Father and Jesus Christ! These mansions prepared for you were constructed by the Master Builder and Maker, Almighty God, and are offered free by Jesus Christ, and you are invited by the Holy Spirit.  No more fears of traveling or worries about things that might happen along our journey through life. No more doctors telling, "You have only six more months to live." Anything that has taken joy out of life and anything that tended to make worship boring on earth has ceased to exist. When we reach our destination, we will celebrate the triumph of God's Kingdom.

The Gospels seriously depict the life of repentance and forgiveness which Christians are to live at all times. Jesus said, "You also must be ready, for the Son of Man will come at an hour when you do not expect Him"(Mk. 12:40).

*1. What will happen on the Last Day according to Matthew 16:27; 25:31-34?*

*2. How do you react to the statement, "Our biggest task is not to prepare for death. Our great task is to prepare for life."?*

1 Cor. 4:5 informs us that Christ will bring to light what is hidden in the dark and reveal people's motives when He comes, and each believer will receive praise from God. Jim Elliot, who died at the hands of the Auca Indians in 1956, made a classic life statement, "He is no fool who give what he cannot keep, to gain what he cannot lose." Repentance is a giving up of something that harms us - that we should not keep. Forgiveness gives us the treasure of eternal life in heaven - that which we cannot lose.

*What is your observation concerning Jim Elliot's statement, "He is no fool who gives what he cannot keep to gain what he cannot lose"?*

The disciples were not to fear what people would do to them, but rather only Him who would be able to destroy both

**Week Fifteen**                                                    **295**

body and soul in hell (Mt. 10:28).  The entire New Testament is filled with the idea that our lives and ethics must stand the test of the Last Times (eschatology).

The "Last Times" message maintains that the present life will not really end at death for the Christian, but will be changed to an eternal dimension.  In Christ our lives will be consummated in glory.  Our faith and actions are directly related to an eternal spiritual realm.  We have no reason to fear death because it has no power over us who will be raised with Christ (1 Cor. 15:54-57).

*1.   How can we be properly prepared for the Last Times?*

*2.   How should the facts of the Last Times affect our personal witnessing and evangelism?*

The signs of the Second Coming of Christ are false christs and false prophets who deceive many, wars, famines, earthquakes, persecutions, increase in wickedness, love of many growing cold, and the Gospel preached in all the world (Mt. 24:4-14).

Christ will return to resurrect all people (believers to glory and unbelievers to hell).  Jesus' Coming will end the existence of the world. The universe will be destroyed and God will create a new heaven and a new earth (2 Pet. 3:12-13).

**Week Fifteen**                                          

*What do the following verses tell us about our existence in Heaven?*

| 1 Cor. 13:12 |  |
|---|---|
| 1 John 3:2<br>Rev. 21:4 |  |
| Rev. 7:15 |  |

We will need no heavenly travel guide, for this is our final destination of glory, where all our blunders are swept away and forgotten. We will celebrate the triumph of God's kingdom, the destruction of evil, and the glory of eternal fellowship with the Father, the Son and the Holy Spirit. Anything that tended to make worship dry and dreary on earth will cease to exist. The eternal strains of music will involve each citizen of heaven in the exaltation of praise.

*Why is the doctrine about the Last Times important for us even if we expect to live another 40 years?*

Our life and the world itself is also coming to an end. We don't need to be afraid of either of these ends. Jesus is coming again, and we will live with Him forever.

Go to God now in prayer and ask Him to give you perfect peace for the time when Jesus comes and you will stand before the judgment seat of Christ. After your time of prayer, spend a minute in silence. Record any thoughts you might have below.

**Week Fifteen**            297

## Day Three -- Waiting in Hope

Through the whole history of the world, God has been carrying out His plan, and will continue to do so until the Last Day. God equips His people to live for His praise and glory in the present age as they look forward in hope toward reaching their permanent home.  Thus people face a constant fierce struggle to carry on the work Jesus gave them to do.  Satan continues to fight hard against God and His people, trying to overthrow the divine plan.  Satan cannot win. Christians live in the sure hope of final victory.

This spiritual guide has shown you the path of life and victory over death.  It has offered very many truths from the Word of Life.  A perfect path of righteousness has been clearly declared.

*What problems can you expect to encounter in your quest for regular Bible study and for joining a lively study group?*

We have looked at the broken paths and the need for restoration.  We have followed the path of Jesus, the Life giver and Restorer.  Baptism was shown to be an entrance to our path of life. We saw the importance of the Law and Gospel in order to walk the path of life with God.  We looked at worship and prayer so that we can keep close to God along the way.  We studied our place in the Christian community, which puts us on the spiritual road with others.

Being prepared for that day means to keep on growing and to look at the opportunities and challenges that lie ahead.  In this journey of faith, you have been learning the Word of God.

*Week Fifteen*                                           298

The Holy Spirit has been helping you to grow spiritually in understanding the Word, and to live as a child of God.

*How are you prepared to live a life of grace and worthy of your calling in Christ?*

Go to God in prayer and thank Him that Jesus' sacrifice is totally sufficient so that our hope is secure for everlasting life with God.  After your time of prayer, spend a minute in silence. Record any thoughts you might have below.

## Day Four -- Lifelong Learning and Growth

Now is the time to develop the habit of reading daily in the Word, not as a duty, but as a means of developing a growing personal relationship with Jesus Christ and our loving Heavenly Father.  This study time should have the highest priority.

Bible study begins with a prayer for understanding by the Holy Spirit and for a willingness to obey and deal with unresolved sin if it is present.

Personal Bible study should be properly planned, not haphazard.  There are great benefits in quiet time with God.  We can apply His Word to our life by asking the following questions: Is there an example for me to follow? Is there a command for me to obey?  Is there a Gospel message to motivate and empower me? Is there any sin for me to avoid or renounce?  Is there any promise for me to claim?  Is there any new insight to guide me?

Bible study must be consistent and systematic.  Just as we eat daily, so we should read or study the Bible regularly.  It is also a great advantage to memorize parts of the Word of God.

We should pray for the Holy Spirit to help us put into practice what we learn.  This starts with willing acceptance of the truth.  A Christian response is characterized by trust, obedience, praise and thanksgiving.  A Bible is not a rule book, but a book that gives life abundantly by the Holy Spirit.

The only way to grow in any relationship is to invest time together.  Time with God in His Word will build your relationship with Him.  Be involved also in Bible study groups where you can learn God's Word together with others.

1.  *What are the key ingredients for taking time for Bible study and a devotional time?*

2.  *What benefits do you expect from developing daily Bible study habits?*

## Day 5 -- Plan Your Next Destination

People usually think of the completion of a Bible study course or any other venture as the end.  If the Spiritual Travel Guide is anything at all, it is a beginning - the beginning of basic knowledge of what Christianity is all about.  It is one big step toward a lifetime of being equipped as a servant and witness of Christ. We have completed the preface to life-long spiritual growth.

**Week Fifteen** 300

This is the moment to plan and work toward growing as a Christian and being equipped as a servant of our awesome God. Our maturity begins with the truth of Rom. 10:10, "It is with your heart that you believe and are justified, and it is with your mouth that you confess and are saved." Your next steps of faith flow from the fact that Jesus is your Lord by the Holy Spirit.

We have seen that all of life is a continuous experience of repentance and forgiveness. Moving toward greater maturity will mean that regularly you will "produce fruit in keeping with repentance"(Lk. 3:8). There should always be a desire for change and growth, sometimes burning in your heart when you face a special problem or mountain.

Half-heartedness and lethargy about spiritual things should be avoided like the plague. Feelings will not be the measurement of how close you are to God, but assurance of God's love for you and your confession that Jesus is your Lord. Having a thirst for God's best, you will pray and pray and pray. Pray for God's presence to guide you.

The Word of God which we have studied these weeks has led us to break away from the carnal values, strongholds and practices of our old nature.

We have come to an end of a short journey into Kingdom thinking and living which leads us to adopt the practice of regular study and meditation on God's Word.

We recognize the need to know God more, to listen to Him daily, and to change values and lifestyle to fit Kingdom living.

Looking at the future, we stand confidently with saving faith for all eternity, and with trusting faith that God is good and will lead us on the paths of righteousness.

As you now look at the journey beyond today, present yourself to God as one who has been called as a servant and witness of the Lord Jesus Christ, and qualified by God's grace to do what God wants and to go where God leads. "...You have been given fullness in Christ, Who is the Head over every power and authority"(Col. 2:10).

Planning for your journey beyond today, describe what you will commit yourself to do in your walk with God as you continue your spiritual travel to greater heights and vistas. If you are not knowledgeable or certain regarding the next step or resource available, discuss it with a spiritual leader and then complete this exercise.


* * * * * * * * * * * * * * * * * * * * * * * * * * *


PLANNING MY FUTURE, I WILL TAKE THE FOLLOWING STEPS WITH THE HELP OF GOD:

| AREA | STEPS I WILL TAKE | MY PRIORITIES |
| --- | --- | --- |
| 1. Bible study | | |
| 2. Personal faith and life | | |
| 3. Home/family | | |
| 4. Social/rela- tionships/ caring | | |

**Week Fifteen**

| 5. | Vocational work | | |
|---|---|---|---|
| 6. | Church service/involvement | | |
| 7. | Financial | | |
| 8. | Prayer | | |
| 9. | Join a small group | | |

**OBSERVATIONS/REFLECTIONS ON WHAT YOU HAVE STUDIED IN THE "SPIRITUAL TRAVEL GUIDE" DURING THE PAST FIFTEEN WEEKS:**

1. What matters or issues would you like to know more about? What, if anything, troubled you about what you studied?

2. What new knowledge or insights have you learned?

3. How has your faith grown or been modified?

4. How will this affect your life?

*Week Fifteen*                                303

# ENCOURAGEMENT TO THE TEACHER/FACILITATOR/LEADER

You have the great privilege of providing direction, encouragement, guidance and leadership as a facilitator for an individual or a group using the **Spiritual Travel Guide**. You help provide a positive atmosphere and good tone for the life of those who will be taking this journey with you. Nothing is so important on the journey of life than to define and understand its purpose and direction, and the resources to reach the destination. This is the goal of this Bible Study.

You and those in your group will develop strong relationships in Christ. People grow as Christians when they learn biblical truth, allow God to shape their inner selves, and respond in action with their lives.

God shapes and molds us into the people He wants us to be through Bible study. The most important thing you can do for those studying with you is to help them experience growth in faith and actions.

Once people experience growth that leads to positive change, they will desire to learn more, and the cycle repeats itself. The advantage of studying together is that you can encourage application in very real and practical ways...Your role will be to make sure that learning includes application through prayer, discussion, modeling and accountability. You are to help build relationships, openness and trust between yourself and the participants.

It is essential that participants write the answers to the questions in the **Spiritual Travel Guide**. Doing so will increase their learning. As you conduct a session, watch carefully to see if the work has been done. This should be obvious as they share their answers to the questions. If they have not completed the work, encourage them to do so before the next meeting.

Every participant is expected to read the contents of the material for each week and write the answers in the book. Do not teach the material in the meeting when you meet, but rather ask the questions and add your own thoughts if you wish, so that the material for that week is covered adequately through the discussion. There is to be no lecturing or even reviewing of the materials, but this is done through writing the answers to the questions by the participants. Using the question approach will keep you from lecturing. Instead, you will be listening to be sure that the participants know the biblical material adequately. You may add your own answer if it is an additional thought when everyone else has completed their reports. Your task is help the participants to apply the truths to their life situations.

A suggested time frame for the meeting is :

| Minutes | Activity |
| --- | --- |
| 5 | Share and pray, asking God for His blessing. |
| 50 | Answer the questions, discuss the material and apply the truths. |
| 5 | Pray for one another and for unsaved friends. |

The first session will be slightly different from the others because it includes some community building. The goal of this session is to develop a closer relationship and common understanding of the journey that you will share. Tell a little about yourself, your work and your spiritual growth, and ask the others to make a brief introduction of themselves, too. As in all the sessions, try to be a facilitator to get others to share the truths and applications of God's Word which will give the participants life-changing experiences. Let prayer permeate every meeting at the beginning and end of each meeting, and also when there are special and specific needs.

# CROSS+BEARERS

The Christian organization, CROSS+BEARERS, is committed to encourage professing Christians to put into practice Jesus' words and example, by being Christ-like in their lifestyle.

In Luke 9:23-24, Jesus gives four requirements for a truly Christian life: "If anyone would come after Me, (1) he must deny himself and (2) take up his cross daily and (3) follow Me. For whoever wants to save his life will lose it, but (4) whoever loses his life for me will save it." Jesus set the example as He was willing and determined to go to Jerusalem, where He would endure suffering and shame, and take up the Cross and carry it to Mount Calvary, where He was crucified.

CROSS+BEARERS are saved by trusting in Jesus as their Savior, who is "the Way and the Truth and the Life"(John 14:6). A CROSS+BEARER seeks to willingly live the way Jesus taught, giving time and resources in loving service to Christ and His people.

Cross-bearing is both voluntary and necessary, consciously taking up our cross daily and carrying it patiently, to give witness to our Christian faith. The cross which Christ asks us to carry is not one that is imposed on us like various afflictions or losses, but a willing service of denying ourselves and sacrificially giving ourselves for the sake of the Gospel. This means saying, "Yes!" to what God desires, and "No!" to our sinful self or flesh. We will no longer live for ourselves, but "live for Jesus who died and rose again for us."

CROSS+BEARERS confess Jesus by words and deeds, telling of Jesus to everyone they meet. They stand firm in the faith, being strong to follow God's will, "do everything in love." 1 Cor. 16:14).

The purpose of the CROSS+BEARERS organization is to encourage Christians to share Jesus Christ, to witness of their faith also by wearing the CROSS+BEARERS pin, and to develop and publish intensive Bible study courses to help deepen the knowledge, faith and actions of Christians.

---

### CROSS+BEARER Membership Request

• Believing in Jesus Christ as my Savior, and seeking to serve Him as my Lord, and

• Having read the CROSS+BEARER statement of purpose and subscribing to our Lord's call to cross-bearing,

I request membership in the CROSS+BEARER organization.

Name: _____________________ Phone: _______________

Address:___________________________State:______Zip: _______

☐  I enclose $5 by check as a gift for the CROSS+BEARER membership pin.

*[Make a copy of this application form and send it with a $5 gift to Mr. Larry Eifler, Treasurer, CROSS+BEARERS, 1135 Grape Street, Denver CO 80220. Phone: (303) 333-6893.]*

# EMPOWERING & MOBILIZING GOD'S PEOPLE
## Discipling Series

Launching New SMALL GROUP BIBLE STUDIES For Leaders & Members To Revitalize Christians And To Renew Churches

## *THE DISCIPLING MODEL*

Disciple-making should be the center of all church activities. Spiritual multiplication and reproduction of believers, not just adding members to the church, was the approach of Jesus and Paul. Jesus said, "Go and make disciples... teaching them to do everything that I have commanded you." (Matt. 28:19-20). Paul said: "We should stop going over the elementary truths about Christ and move on to topics for more mature people." (Hebr. 6:1a GW) Paul told the purpose of Bible study for members: "to prepare God's people for works of service" (Eph. 4:12); for leaders to teach and "entrust to faithful men who will also be able to teach others" (2 Tim. 2:2).

## *THE STRATEGY & SYSTEM*

The "Empowering & Mobilizing God's People" Discipling Series helps mobilize the entire church by equipping God's people through an intensive educational curriculum to activate the priesthood of all believers in the most biblical and practical way. Members are fed and led by God's Word to be totally obedient to Christ's Great Commission. These outstanding interactive educational resources open doors to mobilize Christians to enter many new avenues of Gospel ministry.

Believers are empowered to initiate, lead, and become engaged in the comprehensive, extensive, and all-embracing work which Christ has given them in His church. The laity are empowered to be full participants, not merely spectators or by-standers.

Empowerment is the key. The Discipling Series presents the practical application of Ephesians 4 in the areas of leadership and member development to pursue God's call for greater ministry and mission. It is a lifetime learning process for spiritual growth and discovery, which leads from knowledge and understanding to action. Beginning with information, it takes the participant to spiritual formation and transformation - a living relationship with the living God and fellow believers.

This Discipling Series with the individual courses offers the following benefits:

- Help teachers/facilitators guide the participants/students toward self-discovery and group-discovery for maximum learning and putting their faith into practice – through interactive learning. Teach the heart as well as the head.

- Assist congregations to become Equipping Centers, making the training\empowering of all believers and leaders as a priority.

- Change members from maintenance to mission mentality through renewal Bible studies instead of being pushed by programs. Translate attitudes and mental maps that put believers on a life-long journey of lively discipleship beyond their comfort zone toward enlarged productivity.

- Reclaim the grace of God as the center of Christian lives and congregations, freeing them from the legalism of institutionalism and traditionalism.

- Release all believers for full participation in God's mission through becoming teachers, spiritual leaders, care givers, support group directors, and personal witnesses of Jesus Christ.

## *INTERACTIVE LEADER'S COURSES:*

**God Says Move: Go Where He Leads**, by Waldo J. Werning. Proposes the Mission of God to be all about moving and mapping. Based upon the New Testament model, many barriers to this divine mission are identified as maintenance and institutional restrictions to the mission of today's churches. This book places in sharp focus the historic tension between biblical doctrine and church practice. Christ's Great Commission requires that God's people must be mobile, coming and going, and gathering and scattering to reach everyone everywhere with the saving knowledge of Jesus Christ. World mission leader Ralph D. Winter, in the Foreword writes, "This arresting, tough-minded book empowers the reader ... it's a mission handbook to keep at hand for a long time to come! " With its innovative "Measuring Our Maps" instruments, it is a self-help guide for biblical remapping of congregations. Discussion guides are designed for church leaders, pastors, college and seminary classrooms, and all active Christians.

**21$^{st}$ Century Disciples With A 1$^{st}$ Century Faith**, by Waldo J. Werning. Intensive Bible study course with Resource book, leader's guide and student workbook to build healthy leaders who administer a healthy church. This is the missing niche in the range of educational materials required to make mature and able leaders through interactive learning. Equips leaders with the knowledge and power to give them the winning edge. Lyle D. Muller commends, "A wealth of biblical and practical materials are at the teacher's disposal." The depth of biblical education and application provides a thorough faith-strengthening experience for leaders.  This 26-week course for leaders offers dynamic studies for up to ten participants in a group that meets for about two hours weekly.  Congregations report explosive results.

## *INTERACTIVE SMALL GROUP BIBLE STUDIES/ MEMBERSHIP DEVELOPMENT:*

**"Spiritual Travel Guide,"** by Waldo J. Werning: A fifteen week Bible study course that "takes you on a journey of faith to bring profitable growth and change to your life, beliefs, values, and goals and possibly even the direction you are going.  Think of this Bible study as power-food that fuels you for your life-long adventure with Christ.  You will be shown your credentials, passport, and visa for travel in this foreign country called Earth."  This "Travel Guide" is a map for going on the Great Adventure of life in a relationship with the living God and with fellow Christians.  It presents the music of the Gospel and Word to explode within the believer to give spiritual health and strength that impacts upon all of life.

**"Spiritual Fitness Exercise,"** by Waldo J. Werning: This ten-week small group study resource, which has been field tested with great results, provides guidance for a group of ten or less to build relationships through interactive activities which involve:

- 70 days of personal devotions through the book *Change My Heart, Change My world.*
- Performing weekly kindness/service deeds and sharing experiences.
- Encouraging one another through witnessing and evangelism contacts of at least one person a week for 10 weeks.

- Reading and sharing insights from an educational/ inspirational book, *I Would Really Be Happy If...*
- Excellent follow-up for Promise Keepers.

**"Living Without Slaveries,"** by Waldo J. Werning: This 15-week small group interactive Bible study, which has been field tested in over 75 churches with great success, provides a message of grace/repentance/forgiveness/ spiritual growth and renewal to overcome all kinds of addictions, compulsions, obsessions, and habits which may control and keep us captive as slaves in one way or another. This is a Christian version of the Twelve Step Plan, leading toward healing and reconciliation in order to maintain spiritual health and strength, and building personal relationships. It is an excellent tool to help build support groups in a congregation.

**"The Way To Life,"** by Waldo J. Werning: (Publishing date: August 1998). **"The Way To Life"** involves a 3-hour witnessing seminar, and five weeks of mentoring believers (new and old) in one-on-one sharing their Christian faith with their "Circle of Influence." Provides a new witnessing diagram to share the Way To Life for telling the Good News to non-Christians.

**"Building Christian Community/Relationships In A Healthy Church"**: (Publishing date: December 1998.) Presents eight quality characteristics of a healthy church: Passionate spirituality, inspiring worship services, loving relationships, empowering leadership, gift-centered ministry, holistic small groups, zealous witnessing/gospel-centered evangelism, and functional structures. Action steps include identifying obstacles, determining minimum factors, building spiritual momentum, setting qualitative goals, exercising strength, and monitoring effectiveness. Program multiplication and reproduction principles of the Scriptures are offered.

Fairway Press, P.O. Box 4503, Lima OH 45802-4503, phone: (800) 241-4056. Discipling/Stewardship Center, 1914 Wendmere Lane, Fort Wayne IN 46825, (219) 485-1981 or (219) 484-3524.